Pipe-Major
W. ROSS'S
COLLECTION

OF

HIGHLAND
BAGPIPE
MUSIC

BOOK 2

All tunes in this Book are arranged by
Pipe-Major W. Ross and are copyright.

PATERSON'S PUBLICATIONS
14-15 Berners Street, London W1T 3LJ

Contents.

	Page
Angus Mac Rae, *Reel*	41
Arniston Castle, *Strathspey*	24
Barley Mow, The *Jig*	20 and 46
Black Mill, The *Reel*	45
Bob of Fettercairn, The *Strathspey*	26
Cabar Feidh, *Strathspey*	22
Captain Batchelor, Glasgow Academy	16
Cecily Ross, *Reel*	42
Clan Mac Coll, The *March*	7
Clementina, *Reel*	32
Cluny's Strathspey	29
Colonel Mac Leod, *Strathspey*	28
Crags of Stirling, The *March*	9
Doctor Mac Leod of Alnwick, *March*	5
Donachd Head, *Jig*	20
Duke of Edinburgh, The *Strathspey*	30
Ewe with the Crooked Horn, The *Strathspey*	21
Helmsdale Fishers, The *Jig*	19
Jamie Ray, *Jig*	20
John Mac Coll's Farewell to the Scottish Horse, *March*	8
John Mac Gregor Murray's March	4
John Morrison Esq. of Assynt House, *March*	14
John Paterson's Mare, *Jig*	17
Kilberry Castle, *March*	6
Lady Madelina Sinclair, *Strathspey*	29
Leaving Port Askaig, *March*	13
Leaving St. Kilda, *Slow Air*	30
Loch an Dùin, *Reel*	31
Lochiel's away to France, *Reel*	33
Lonach Gathering, The *March*	3
Lord Alexander Kennedy, *March*	10
Lord Mac Donald, *Reel*	38
Mac Beth's Strathspey	23
Mac Lennan's Overcoat, *Strathspey*	28
Maggie Cameron, *Strathspey*	25
Maids of Kintail, The *March*	12
Malcolm Johnston, *Reel*	34
Mo Chuachag Laghach Thu, *Reel*	31
Mrs. Pat Mac Laren, *March*	1
Old Ruins, The *Reel*	44
Over the Isles to America, *Reel*	35
Pandora's Reel	32
Pipe Major W. Ross's Welcome to Sutherland, *March*	15
Sandy Cameron, *Reel*	39
Seventy First's Highlanders, The *March*	2
Sheepwife, The *Reel*	36
Shepherd's Crook, The *Strathspey*	27
Smith of Chilliechassie, The *Reel*	40
"Theid mi dhachaidh 'chrò chinn t-sàile" *Slow Air*	45
Thomson's Dirk, *Reel*	43
Willie the Tailor, *Jig*	19

Mrs. Pat MacLaren. **March.** By P.M. W. Ross.

The 71st's Highlanders.

March.

By Hugh MacKay

The Lonach Gathering. March.

By W. Grant, late Scots Gds

John MacGregor Murray's March.

By P.M. R. Meldrum.

Doctor MacLeod of Alnwick. March.

By P.M. A. Ross, late Scots Gds.

Kilberry Castle.

March.

By Archibald Campbell, Kilberry.

The Clan MacColl.*   March.

By John MacColl.

*With kind permission of the Clan MacColl Society.

John MacColl's Farewell to the Scottish Horse. March.

By John MacColl.

The Crags of Stirling. March.

By Hugh MacKay.

Lord Alexander Kennedy.   March.

By J. Honeymon 42nd Highlanders.

The Maids of Kintail. March.

Leaving Port Askaig. March.

W. Ross.

John Morrison Esq. of Assynt House. March.

By Pipe Major W. Ross.

Pipe Major W. Ross's Welcome to Sutherland. March.

By A. MacPherson, Inveran.

Captain Batchelor Glasgow Academy.

J. MacColl.

John Paterson's Mare.

Jig.

Willie the Tailor.

Jig.

The Helmsdale Fishers.

Jig.

Jamie Ray. **Jig.**

Donachd Head. **Jig.**

The Barley Mow. **Jig.** J. Graham Campbell, Shirvan.

For Parts 3 and 4 see page 46.

The Ewe with the Crooked Horn.

Strathspey.

Cabar Feidh.

Strathspey.

Mac Beth's Strathspey. Strathspey.

Arniston Castle.   **Strathspey.**

Maggie Cameron. Strathspey.

The Bob of Fettercairn.

Strathspey.

The Shepherd's Crook. Strathspey.

MacLennan's Overcoat.   Strathspey.

Colonel Mac Leod.   Strathspey.

Lady Madelina Sinclair.   **Strathspey.**

Cluny's Strathspey.

The Duke of Edinburgh. Strathspey.

Leaving St. Kilda. Slow Air.

By P M. W. Ross.

Mo Chuachag Laghach Thu.   Reel

Loch an Dùin.   Reel

Pandora's Reel.

By J. Graham Campbell, Shirvan.

Clementina. Reel.

Lochiel's away to France.   Reel.

Malcolm Johnston. Reel.

By Rod. Campbell.

Over the Isles to America.   Reel.

The Sheepwife. Reel.

Lord Mac Donald.   Reel.

Sandy Cameron.   **Reel.**

The Smith of Chilliechassie.   Reel.

Angus Mac Rae.   Reel.

Cecily Ross. Reel. R. Campbell.

Thomson's Dirk.   Reel.

44

The Old Ruins.　　Reel.

"Theid mi dhachaidh 'chrò chinn t-sàile"   Slow Air.

The Black Mill.   Reel.

The Barley Mow.   Jig.   *Part 3 and 4.*

BAGPIPE MUSIC FROM THE PATERSON CATALOGUE

LOGAN'S BAGPIPE TUTOR *

LOGAN'S COLLECTION BOOK 1

ROSS'S COLLECTION BOOKS 1 to 5

ARMY MANUAL OF PIPE TUNES AND DRUM BEATINGS BOOKS 1 AND 2

THE PIPER'S DELIGHT

QUEEN'S OWN HIGHLANDERS STANDARD SETTINGS

SCOTS GUARDS STANDARD SETTINGS... PAPER COVERS

SCOTS GUARDS STANDARD SETTINGS... CLOTH BOARDS

BAGPIPE MUSIC FOR DANCING *

MORE MUSIC FOR THE HIGHLAND BAGPIPE *

CEOL BEAG AGUS CEOL MOR (Little Music and Big Music) *

THE PIPER'S HANDBOOK — A NON-MUSICAL GUIDE *

Written or edited by Pipe-Major John MacLellan

PATERSON'S PUBLICATIONS

EXCLUSIVELY DISTRIBUTED BY

DISTRIBUTED BY HAL LEONARD

8 84088 42740 5

14027838

Order No: PAT30052

ISBN 978-0-85360-248-4

9 780853 602484

The Gig Bag Book of

ALTERNATE TUNINGS

for all Guitarists

Over 30 tunings for all guitarists presented in standard notation and tablature.

by Woody Mann

Music Sales America

DISTRIBUTED BY

HAL•LEONARD® CORPORATION

7777 W. BLUEMOUND RD. P.O. BOX 13819 MILWAUKEE, WI 53213

Gretsch Rancher on cover owned by Scot Arch
Cover photograph by William Draffen
Project editor: Ed Lozano
Interior design and layout: Len Vogler

Order No. AM 931271
US International Standard Book Number: 0.8256.1490.2
UK International Standard Book Number: 0.7119.5128.4

Exclusive Distributors:
Music Sales Corporation
257 Park Avenue South, New York, NY 10010 USA
Music Sales Limited
8/9 Frith Street, London W1V 5TZ England
Music Sales Pty. Limited
120 Rothschild Street, Rosebery, Sydney, NSW 2018, Australia

Printed in the United States of America by
Vicks Lithograph and Printing Corporation

Contents

Organizing the Tunings 5

The Chords and Scales 9
The Chords 9
The Chords In Scales 10
A note on picking technique 11

Drop D D A D G B E 13
Amazing Grace 16
Blues In Drop D 17

Related Tunings 19
D A D G B D 19
Amazing Grace 22

Open D D A D F♯ A D 23
Amazing Grace 26
Blues In Vestapol (Open D) 27

Related Tunings 29
Open E E B E G♯ B E 29
D A D G A D 29
Amazing Grace 31
D A D E A D 31
Etude in DADEAD 33

Open D Minor D A D F A D 35
Etude in D Minor 38
Blues in Cross-Note 39

Related Tunings 41
Open E minor E B E G B E 41

Open G D G D G B D 43
Amazing Grace 46
Blues in Spanish 47

Related Tunings 49
Open A E A E A C♯ E 49
D G D G B E "Drop DG" 49
Blues In D 51
Blues in G 52
G B D G B D 53
D G D G A D 54
Song in D G D G A D 55
D G D G C D 55

Open G Minor D G D G B♭ D 57
Melody in Gm 60
Blues in Spanish Minor 61

Related Tunings 63
Open A minor E A E A C E 63

OPEN C C G C G C E **65**
    AMAZING GRACE 67

RELATED TUNINGS **69**
    Drop C C A D G B E 69
    Drop CG C G D G B E 70
       AMAZING GRACE 71
    C Spanish C G D G B D 72
       BLUES IN SPANISH C 74
    C G D G A D 75
    C G C G A E 76

OPEN C MINOR C G C G C E♭ **79**
    C MINOR WALTZ 81

FURTHER POSSIBILITIES **83**
    Lute Tuning E A D F♯ B E 83
    Perfect 4th Tuning E A D G C F 83

OPEN CHORD TUNINGS **85**
    D7 D A D F♯ C D 85
    G7 D G D F B D 85
    Gmaj7 D G D F♯ B D 85
    Dmaj7 D A D F♯ A C♯ 85
    Gm7 D G D F B♭ D 85
    Dm7 D A D F A C 86
    Am7 E A E G C E 86
    Em7 E B D G B E 86

TWO-NOTE TUNINGS **87**
    D A D D A D 87
    D G D D G D 87
    E A E E A E 87
    E B E E B E 87

DISCOGRAPHY **89**
    Traditional Country Blues 89
       Anthologies 93
    Hawaiian 94
       Anthologies 96
    Celtic 96
       Anthologies 98
    Rock, Folk, and the Contemporary
    Stylists 98
       Anthologies 110

ORGANIZING THE TUNINGS

Alternate tunings have become part of the arsenal of sounds that contemporary guitarists have in their repertoire of techniques. Its use in rock, folk, jazz, blues, and country music has established the idea of open tunings as a basic ingredient in the definition of modern guitar language.

Although the use of open tunings is not a new concept-guitar players have been using them since the turn of the century–contemporary musicians have been experimenting and stretching the boundaries. Some open tunings have evolved through a specific musical tradition: Open D and open G tunings, for example, became the stock in trade of the country blues players, and these and other alternate tunings became the basis for the rich tradition of Hawaiian guitar music. Other innovations are a result of one artist simply experimenting and discovering a new way to explore the guitar.

The goal of this manual is serve as a basic first reference guide for alternate tunings. New tunings are constantly evolving so the difficult part of organizing the material was deciding what and how many tunings to include, and a way to present them in a workable format. I wanted to make the information as practical as possible without getting bogged down with a lot of theory. I chose to illustrate in detail the tunings that are used extensively, and have become the 'standards' of alternate tunings. I also listed other variations that guitarists are experimenting with.

Since the open tunings evolved from many diverse sources, there is no standard terminology for the subject. Even the terms 'open' and 'alternate' can have different meanings to guitar players. For example, to some blues musicians, open G is referred to as an open tuning while some call it an alternate tuning. Any formation of the open strings can be spelled to form a variety of chords and tonalities–they are all "open," and at the same time "alternate." Sometimes players make the distinction between root tunings–those with the root of the open chord in the bass (the sixth string–as in open D) and non-root tunings–tunings with a tone of the chord other than the root in the bass (as in open G). Even the names of the tunings are

5

varied. In Hawaiian music, for example, the term *slack key* is a generic name for altered tunings commonly used in guitar music, and each specific tuning has its own name. For example, D G D G B D is sometimes called *Taro Patch tuning*. The same tuning in blues circles is referred to as *Spanish tuning*.

To avoid getting bogged down in semantics–and in order to organize the material into a workable format–I have broadly grouped the tunings in the following categories (chapter headings):**Open Tunings** and **Related Tunings.**

Open tunings refer to those tunings that form an open major or minor chord. In other words, when all six strings are strummed open (without fretting any notes), a major or minor chord is produced. I did not make the distinction between root and non-root tunings.

The *related tunings* are ones in which the open strings produce chords other than pure major or minor chords. Since many of these tunings are tonally related to (in the same key as) the open tunings and share many of the characteristics, I grouped them in the appropriate chapter.

I also listed many of the tunings under the heading of *Further Possibilities.* Along with the lute tuning and perfect 4th tuning, these form other open chords such as major 7, dominant 7, and minor 7. I also included a few tunings that comprise just two notes, implying an undefined tonality and having a drone-like quality. The tunings listed in this chapter are just a few examples of the (limitless?) possibilities for further exploration.

For the tunings I illustrated:

1. How to tune from standard tuning.

2. The basic chord types and positions as well as additional chords that work well in the tuning. In some instances I wrote out the same chord blocks two ways–with and without the open strings. This is to illustrate how the name and sound of chord changes when adding these additional open notes. I also notated the moveable chords.

3. For the open tunings, or the tunings that form a major or minor tonality, I wrote out the diatonic chords (the natural chords in a key) throughout the scale to illustrate the relationship between the chord and the overall tonality. Also shown are the same chords implied by only two notes. This gives you some

ideas about the unique way harmonies work in open tunings.

4. I arranged the song "Amazing Grace," or an original song, to illustrate some of the unique sounds and basic chord positions of the tuning. In the tunings that are used extensively in blues I wrote out a twelve-bar blues verse using familiar riffs and turn-arounds. It is valuable to see how the various tunings affect the same melody and chord progression.

To get the feel of leaving standard tuning, start off with the tunings that are close to standard, such as Drop D or Drop C. Then move on to open D and open G tunings, as these are by far the most used and can be found in the broadest range of guitar styles. They work well with fingerstyle techniques and are the main tunings for blues and rock bottleneck playing. Also, there are many recordings available (see discography) and more printed music for these than any of the other tunings.

As you experiment with these new sounds, it may seem a bit overwhelming and complicated at first. But there is a simplicity to them that soon becomes apparent. The fact is, that in the blues tradition, open tunings were used to teach beginners how to play the guitar. Songs were easy to play because all you had to do was to fret the melody on one string while strumming the other strings open. Richard 'Hacksaw' Harney, the great Mississippi blues musician, once mentioned to me that when he first began to learn guitar, he was shown a few licks in open tuning. "But," he said, "that was too easy... I graduated to standard tuning."

Playing through the tunings in this book has given me new ideas for my own playing—I hope it helps you get the creative wheels turning and the material provides a basis toward further exploration.

Thanks to Joe Ravo and Jeff Dedrick for their help with the project. Thanks to Victor Eisenberg for his work organizing the discography and his valuable assistance.

Good luck,
Woody Mann

THE CHORDS AND SCALES

The Chords

Aside from the basic chords, I have also included many *moveable positions*. These are chords that can be moved in their full form up and down the neck to form other chord names. For the chords that are easily moveable, I have circled the *root* (the note name of the chord). As you slide the shape up, whatever note is fretted on the circled string is the name of the chord. For instance:

In drop D tuning (DADGBE), play the following G chord:

The circled note is the root (or the name of the chord). When you move the position up or down the neck, whatever note is on the circled string is the new name for the chord. So if you move this position up a *whole-step*, or two frets, the chord becomes A major:

A

7fr

The more a chord uses open strings the more difficult it becomes to move,

It is also useful to see how the sound and spelling (or name) of a chord can change when played with open strings. The basic chord type is the same, but the addition of these notes adds alterations and color tones to the chord. For example, if you play the same G chord and add the open 1st string (E), it becomes G major 6th:

G6

The Chords In Scales

In the chord-scale exercises I have written out the *diatonic* triads (the chords in a key) through a key. These are the chords that are built on each tone of the scale.

For example:
Here is the scale of D written out in Drop D (DADGBE) tuning:

D major scale

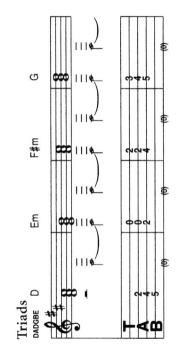

Here are the *natural* (diatonic) chords built on each scale tone. These are the diatonic chords in the key:

Triads

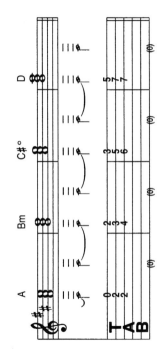

I have notated the root note of the scale (the low D open string, in this case) in cue notes. If you play these optional notes you can hear the relationship between the chord and the root scale tone.

In the major and minor open tunings I also illustrated the chords implied by two notes. These two notes outline the chord (root and third). One of the unique advantages of playing harmonies in open tunings is that it can easily enable you to play only a few notes to state a chord. These interval diagrams illustrate this. As with the triads I notated the root tone of the scale in cue notes.

For example:

Two-note voicings

DADGBE   (D)   (Em)   (F#m)   (G)

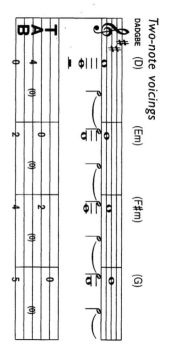

(A)   (Bm)   (C#°)   (D)

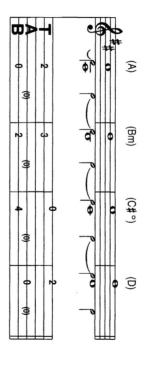

A note on picking technique

Since this book is a reference for tunings—and not a technique guide for picking—I kept the musical examples simple. The melodies, blues verses, and etudes are written within a simple two-line picking pattern without a lot of confusing syncopations. Most times the root of the chord is in the bass (played with the thumb) and the melody is in the top line (played with the fingers). Try playing the pieces very slowly, letting the open strings sustain against the chords. Let the open sounds dictate your playing rather than picking in a set pattern.

DROP D DADGBE

This is a good place to begin to get the feel of altered tunings because only one string is altered from standard.

How to tune from standard:
1st
2nd
3rd
4th
5th
6th lower one whole-step to D

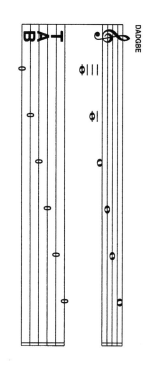

DADGBE

All chord shapes on the first five strings will be the same as the ones fretted in standard tuning.

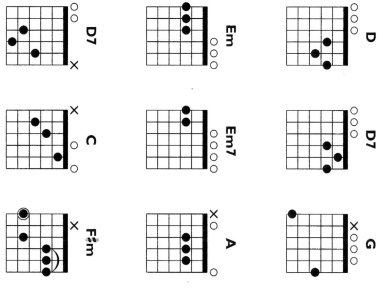

D

D7

G

Em

Em7

A

D7

C

F#m

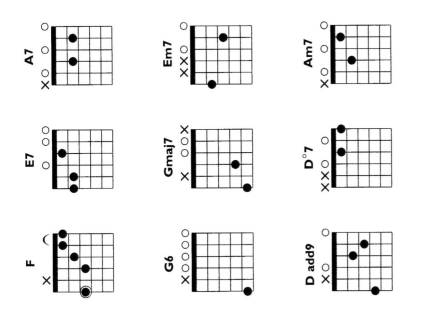

A7

E7

F

Em7

Gmaj7

G6

Am7

D°7

D add9

Although other keys work well in this tuning, songs in the key of D major or D minor are very strong because of the low D in the bass.

The following example illustrates the diatonic chords in the key of D major. Try playing the chords with the *tonic note* (the open sixth string) of the scale to hear the relationship between the chord and the overall modality of the scale.

Triads

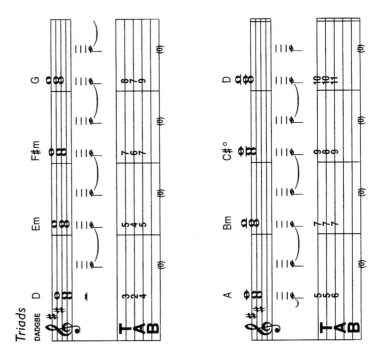

In the next diagram, I illustrated the same chords using two notes (root and third) of the chord. The root (or tonic) tone of the scale is notated in parenthesis.

Two-note voicings

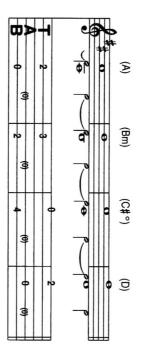

Following are an arrangement of the song "Amazing Grace" and a twelve-bar blues verse, both in drop D tuning.

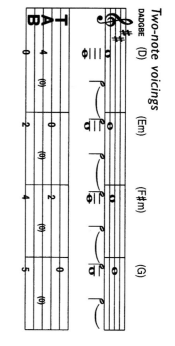

Amazing Grace

DADGBE Slowly

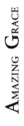
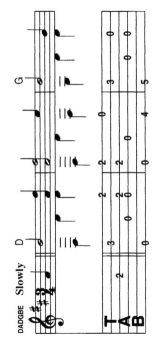

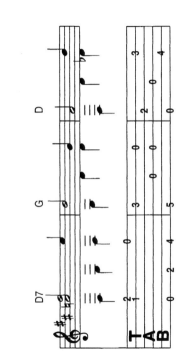
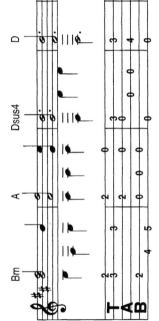

Blues In Drop D

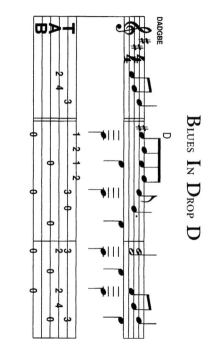
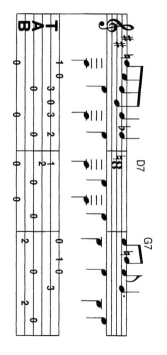
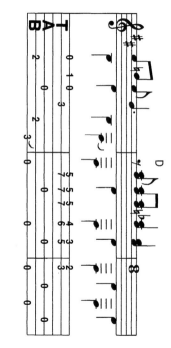
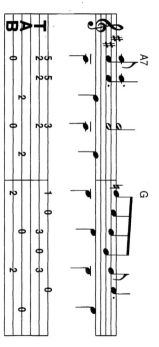
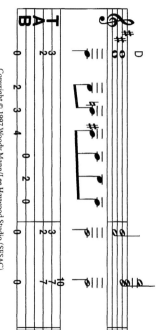

D A D G B D

In this tuning the two E strings are lowered one whole-step to D. This is sometimes referred to as (appropriately enough) *double drop D tuning*.

How to tune from standard:
1 lower one whole-step to D
2
3
4
5
6 lower one whole-step to D

Double drop D tuning staff
DADGBD

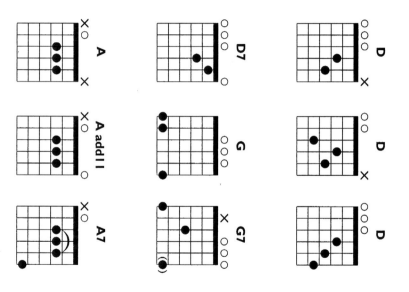

A

A add 11

A7

D7

G

G7

D

D

D

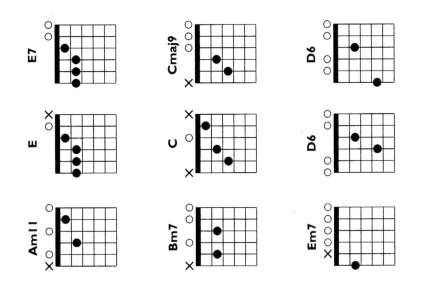

Here are the triads in the key of D:

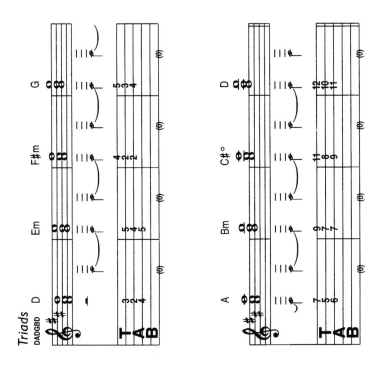

The same chords implied by two notes: The chords implies by two notes (with root of scale in parenthesis)

Two-note voicings

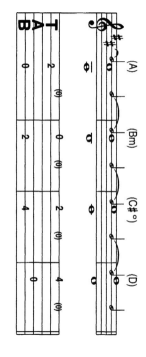

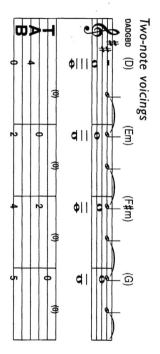

Amazing Grace

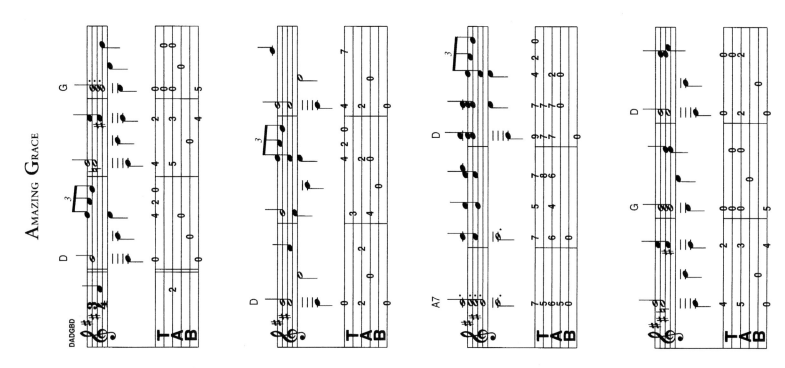

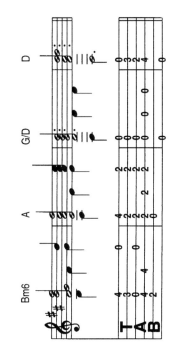

22

OPEN D DADF#AD

Open D tuning is one of the 'standard' open tunings, and it has been used by guitarists since the turn of the century. Many of the great blues artists—from fingerstylists Bo Carter, John Hurt, and Memphis Minnie to bottleneck greats like Robert Johnson, Muddy Waters, and Blind Willie Johnson—played in open D. Sometimes referred to as *Vestapol* tuning, the open strings produce a strong D major chord because the root of the chord is on the sixth string.

How to tune from standard:
1 lower one whole-step to D
2 lower one whole-step to A
3 lower one half-step to F#
4
5
6 lower one whole-step to D

Open D tuning staff

DADF#AD

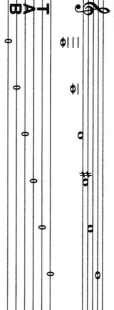

The following diagram illustrates the names of the chords when barring all six strings on a single fret.

Sixth-string root bar chords

DADF#AD   Dmaj   D#maj   Emaj   Fmaj

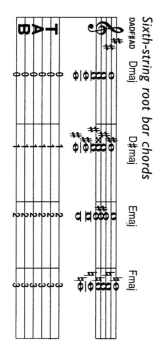

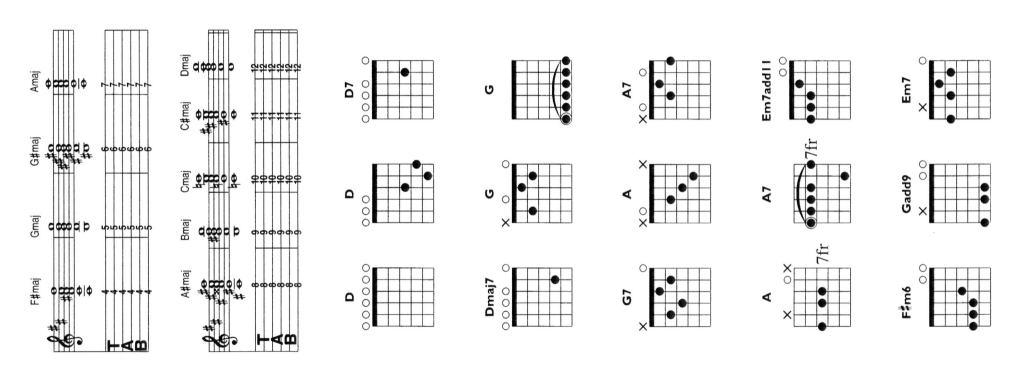

Here are the *triads* (chords) in the key of D. Play these against the open strings in cue notes to hear the root tone of the scale against the chords.

Triads

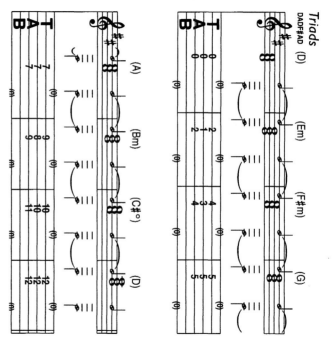

The same chords implied by two notes:

Two-note voicings

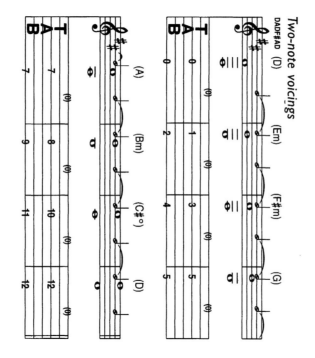

In the following musical examples I wrote out the song "Amazing Grace" and a twelve-bar blues - both using many of the basic chord positions and blues phrases.

25

AMAZING GRACE

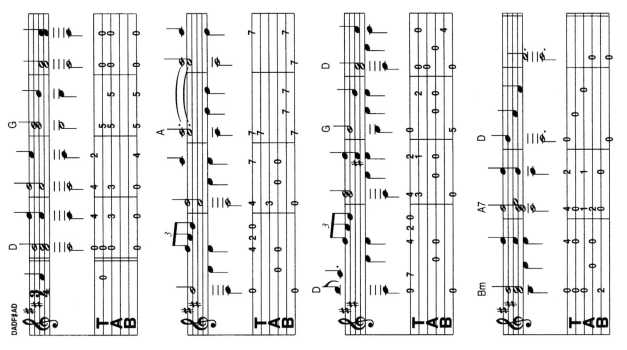

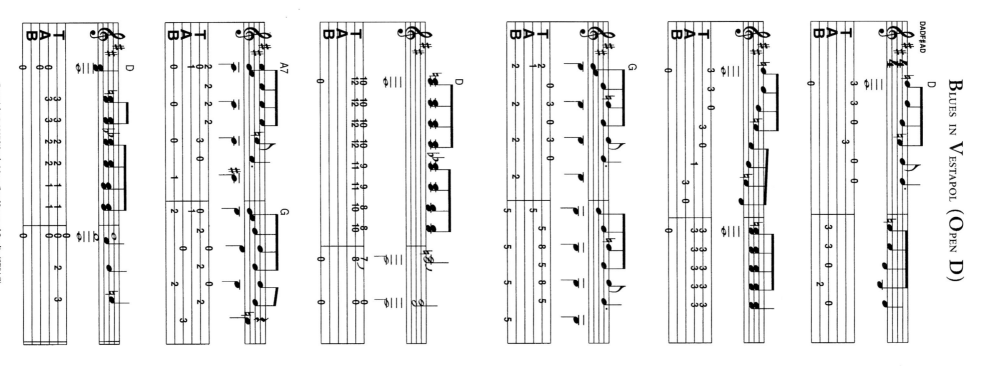

BLUES IN VESTAPOL (OPEN D)

27

RELATED TUNINGS

Open E E B E G# B E

Open E has the same interval relationships among the strings as open D tuning. In other words, all the chord shapes and scales are fingered the same way, and the tablature is identical to open D tuning. The difference is that each string is pitched one whole-step higher, so together they form an E major chord.

How to tune from standard:

1
2
3 raise one half-step to G#
4 raise one whole-step to E
5 raise one whole-step to B
6

Open E tuning staff
EBEG#BE

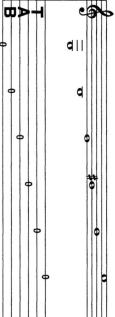

D A D G A D

The open strings of this tuning form a D suspended chord. Because of the missing third of the chord, it produces an undefined tonality—neither major or minor. British guitarist Davey Graham is credited for having come up with this tuning—and it has become one of the most popular tunings for playing Celtic music.

How to tune from standard:

1 lower one whole-step to D
2 lower one whole-step to A
3
4
5
6 lower one whole-step to D

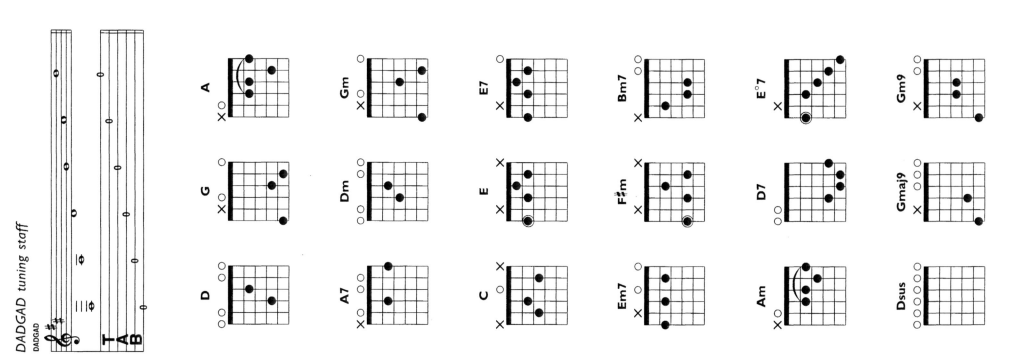

DADGAD tuning staff

DADGAD

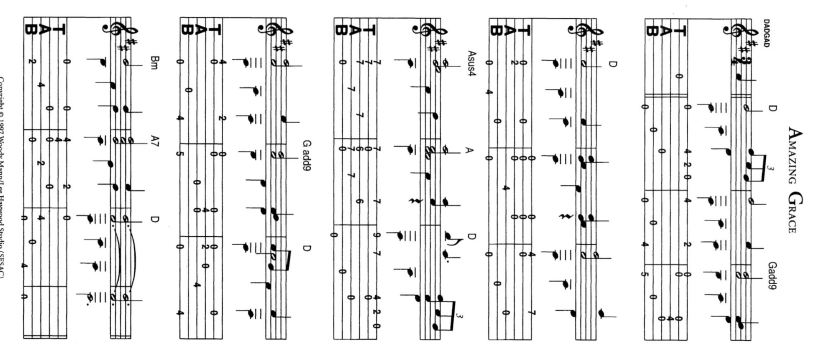

AMAZING GRACE

DADGAD

DADEAD

DADEAD is related to DADGAD–the only difference is that the third string is tuned down to E. Also, like DADGAD this tuning does not imply a major or minor tonality. Songs in the key of D major and D minor both lay comfortably in this tuning. The drone-like, suspended quality makes it a favorite among Celtic guitarists.

How to tune from standard:

1 lower one whole-step to D
2 lower one whole-step to A
3 lower one whole-step and a half to E
4
5
6 lower one whole-step to D

DADEAD tuning staff
DADEAD

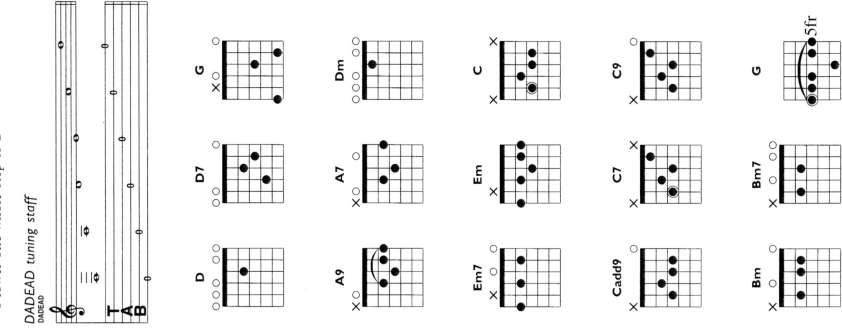

G Dm C C9 G 5fr

D7 A7 Em C7 Bm7

D A9 Em7 Cadd9 Bm

The following musical example is a sixteen-bar song that showcases some of the unique chord positions and sounds of DADEAD tuning.

Etude in DADEAD

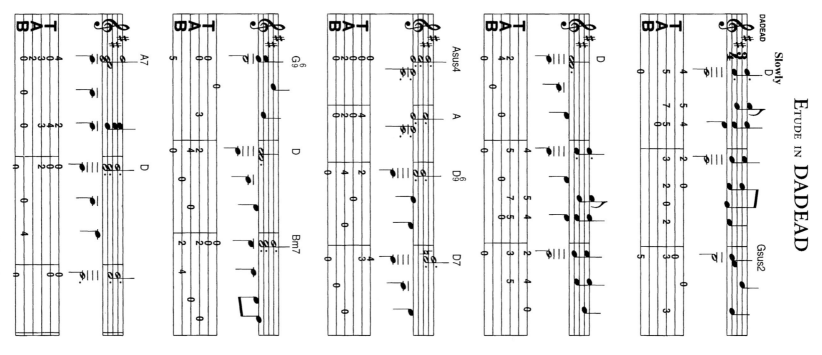

33

OPEN D MINOR
DADFAD

The open strings in this tuning forms a *D minor chord.*

The open third string (the F♮) is the minor third of the chord and when fretted on the first fret, a D major chord is produced. This way it is possible to move in and out of a major or minor tonality very easily–an idea basic in blues music. Because of this feature, blues players dubbed it *cross-note tuning.* Listen to the great blues players who featured cross-note in their guitar playing such as Skip James and Henry Townsend.

How to tune from standard:

1 lower one whole-step to D
2 lower one whole-step to A
3 lower one whole-step to F
4
5
6 lower one whole-step to D

Open D minor tuning staff
DADFAD

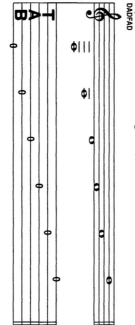

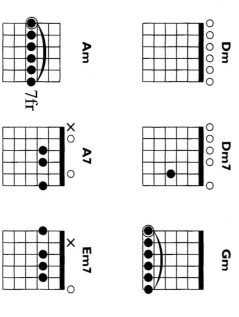

Dm

Dm7

Gm

Am   7fr

A7

Em7

35

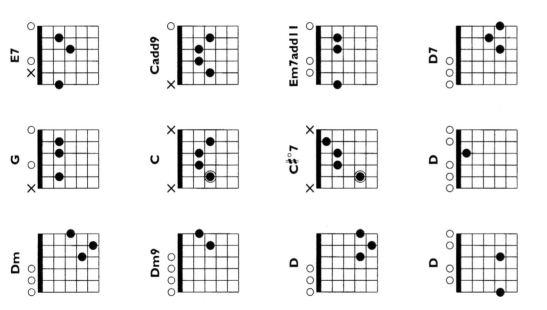

Here are the natural (diatonic) chords through the key of D (natural) minor:

Triads

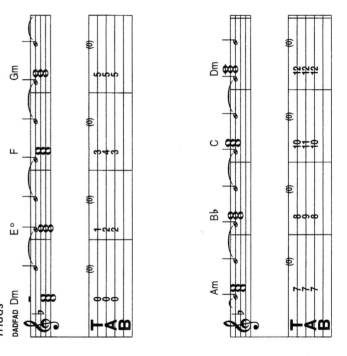

The two-note chords:

Two-note voicings

DADFAD (Dm)

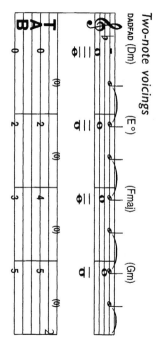

The following etude uses the basic (I, IV, V) chords in the key of D minor.

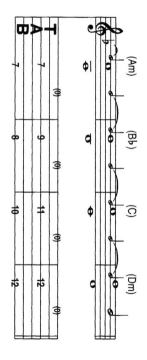

E<small>TUDE IN</small> D <small>MINOR</small>

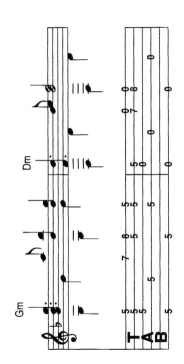

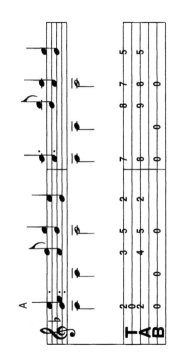

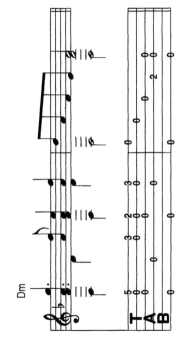

The following twelve-bar blues is notated in the key of D minor, but the *tonality* (the key) of the tune shifts in and out of D major.

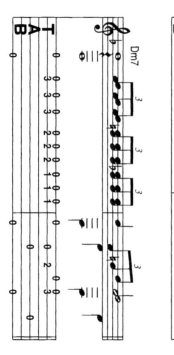

RELATED TUNINGS

Open E minor E B E G B E

Open E minor has the same interval relationships among the strings as open D minor tuning—so the chord shapes, scales, and riffs are fingered the same. The only difference is that the strings are pitched one whole-step higher – to form the E minor chord. The tablature for the "Etude in D minor" and "Blues in Cross-Note" is the same for this tuning.

How to tune from standard:

1
2
3
4 raise one whole-step to E
5 raise one whole-step to B
6

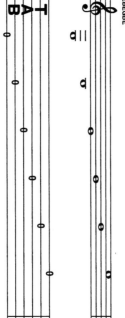

Open E minor tuning staff
EBEGBE

OPEN G D G D G B D

This is probably the most used open tuning. Blues players used this tuning extensively, dubbing it *spanish tuning*. It is also one of the main musical pallettes in Hawaiian guitar music, sometimes referred to it as *taro patch tuning*.

The versatility of the tuning is evidenced by its use in many diverse styles including blues slide playing, fingerstyle, ragtime, Hawaiian music, and contemporary songwriters.

I have arranged "Amazing Grace" as well as a twelve-bar blues that illustrates many of the basic chord formations and riffs.

How to tune from standard:
1 lower one whole-step to D
2
3
4
5 lower one whole-step to G
6 lower one whole-step to D

Open G tuning staff
DGDGBD

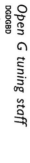

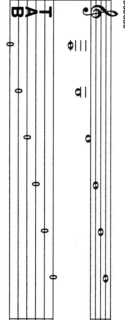

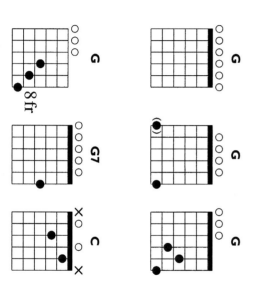

43

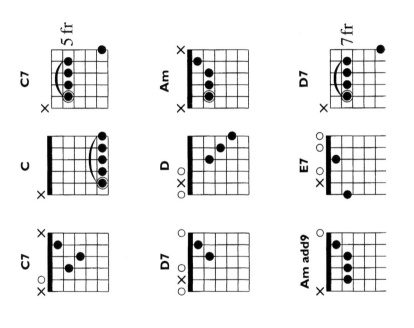

The chords through the scale:

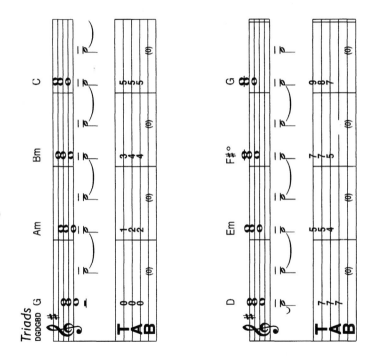

The same chords illustrated by two notes:

Two-note voicings

DGDGBD (G)

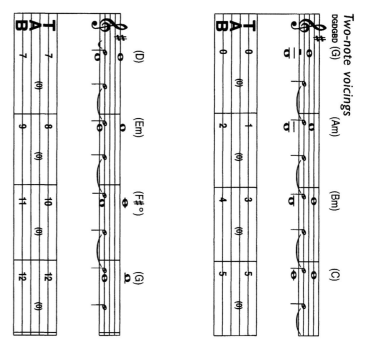

Amazing Grace

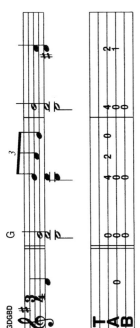
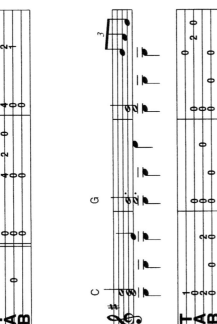
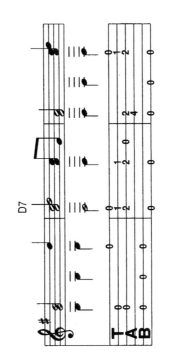
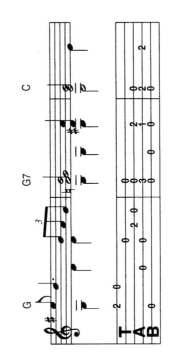
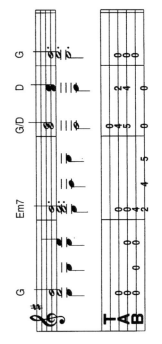

46

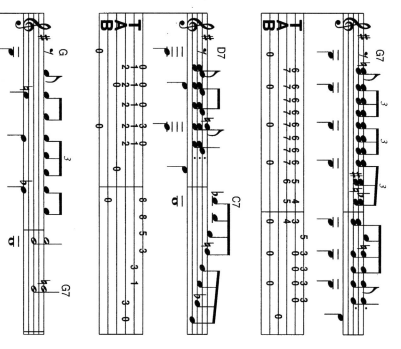
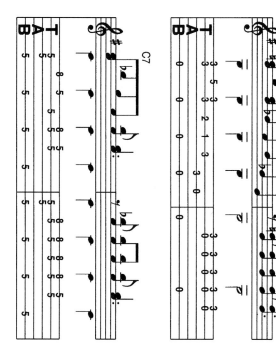
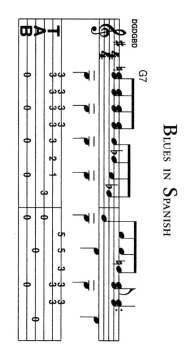

BLUES IN SPANISH

RELATED TUNINGS

Open A E A E A C♯ E

This tuning has the same interval relationships among the strings as open G, but it is pitched a step higher. Play as if you were in open G—the chord shapes and the tablature can be played the same way. (The chord names and the standard notation, of course, would need to be transposed a wholestep up—to the key of A).

How to tune from standard:

1
2 raise one whole-step to C♯
3 raise one whole-step to A
4 raise one whole-step to E
5
6

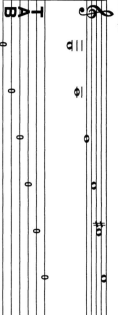

Open A tuning staff
EAEAC♯E

D G D G B E "Drop DG"

In drop DG the two low strings are lowered to give you the root tone of the key of G and D—so those two keys work well in this tuning. I have written out two twelve-bar blues verses in both keys to give you the idea of the possibilities. The chord formations on the top four strings are played the same way as in standard tuning.

How to tune from standard:

1
2
3
4
5 lower one whole-step to G
6 lower one whole-step to D

49

Drop DG tuning staff

DGDGBE

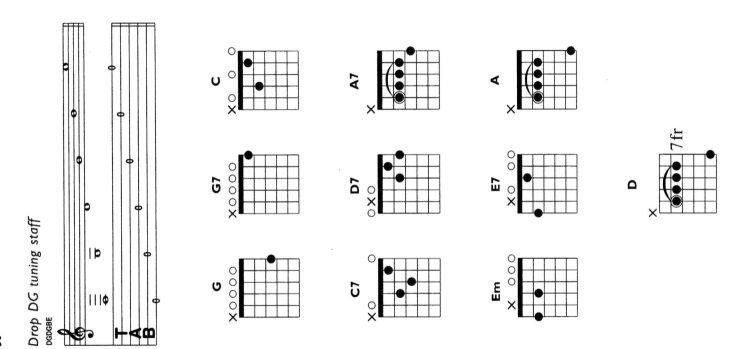

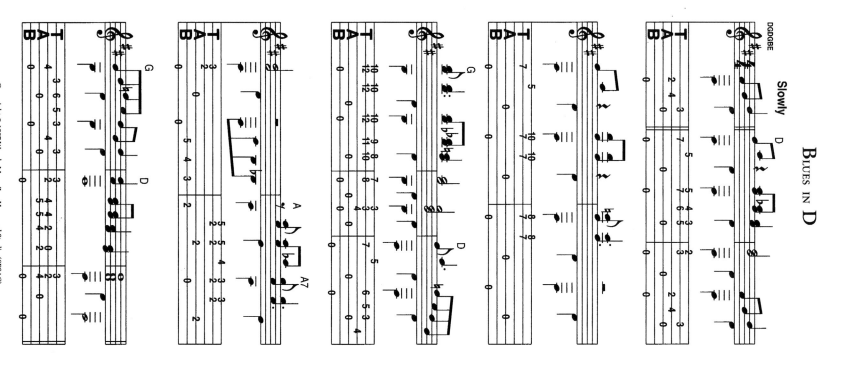

Blues in D

Slowly

DGDGBE

51

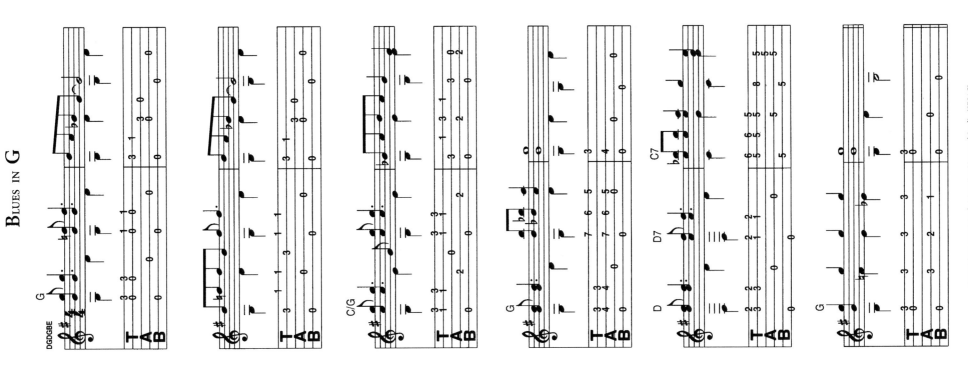

Blues in G

52

G B D G B D

This is a fun tuning because the chord blocks on the top three strings are the same shape as on the bottom three. This is another open major chord tuning like open G—now the root of the chord is in the bass. It is sometimes refered to as *Dobro tuning*.

How to tune from standard:
1 lower one whole-step to D
2
3
4
5 raise one whole-step to B
6 raise one whole-step and a half to G

Open G (dobro) tuning staff
GBDGBD

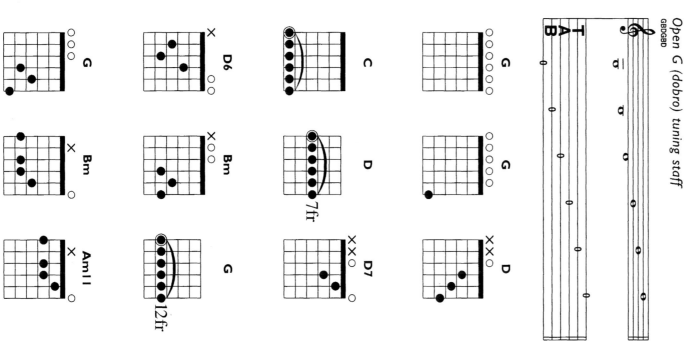

G

G

G

C

7fr

D

D

D7

G

D6

Bm

Bm

G

12fr

G

Bm

Am11

D G D G A D

This tuning is similar to DADGAD except for the lowered fifth string. It has the same suspended quality (Dsus4) but the low G makes it comfortable to play in the key of G. I wrote out the musical example using the basic I, IV, V chords of both the keys of G and D. It begins in G then ends in D.

How to tune from standard:
1 lower one whole-step to D
2 lower one whole-step to A
3
4
5 lower one whole-step to G
6 lower one whole-step to D

DGDGAD tuning staff
DGDGAD

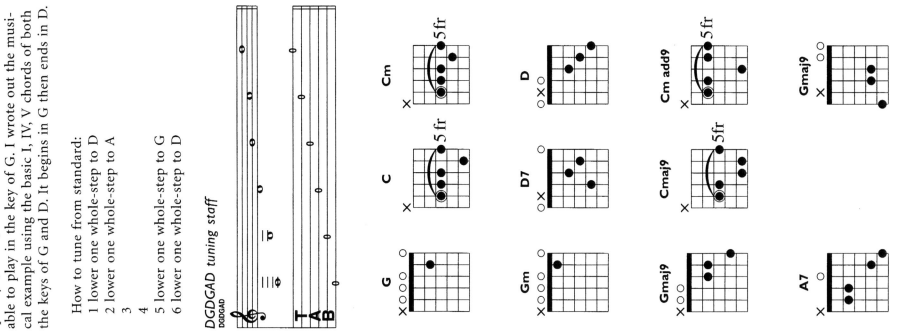

Song in D G D G A D

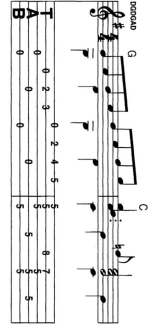

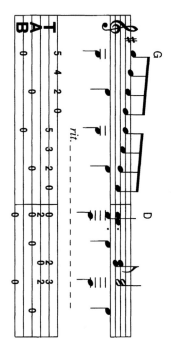

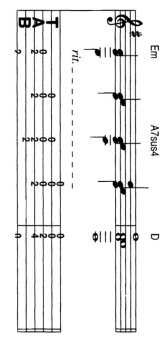

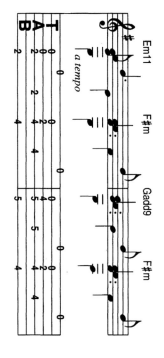

D G D G C D

This is another variation of Spanish tuning except that the tonality is less defined because of the C note on the second string--changing the open strings from forming a major chord to a suspended tonality.

How to tune from standard:
1 lower one whole-step to D
2 raise one half-step to C
3
4
5 lower one whole-step to G
6 lower one whole-step to D

DGDGCD tuning staff

DGDGCD

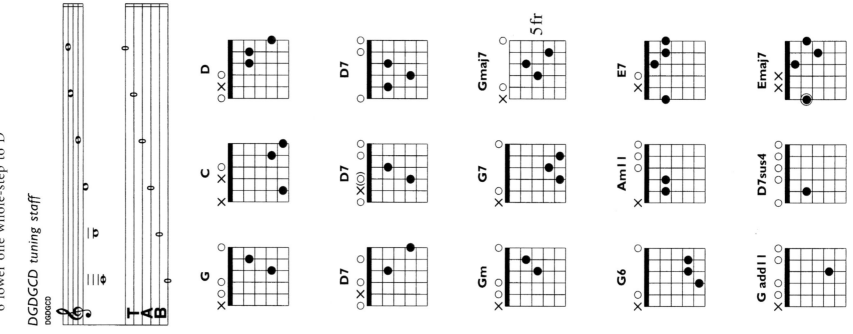

D

C

G

D7

D7

D7

Gmaj7   5 fr

G7

Gm

E7

Am11

G6

Emaj7

D7sus4

G add11

OPEN G MINOR
D G D G B♭ D

The open strings in this tuning form a G minor chord. The lowered second string (B♭) is the only difference from open G (major) tuning—so it is practical to change from a minor to a major tonality easily.

How to tune from standard:
1 lower one whole-step to D
2 lower one half-step to B♭
3
4
5 lower one whole-step to G
6 lower one whole-step to D

Open G minor tuning staff
DGDGB♭D

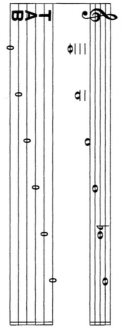

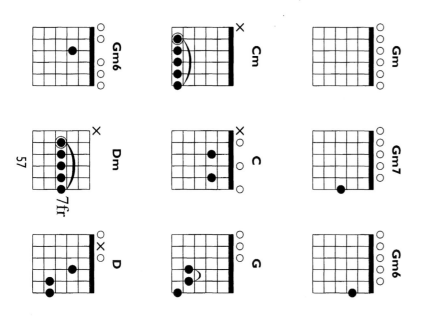

Gm

Gm7

Gm6

Cm

C

G

Gm6

Dm 7fr

D

57

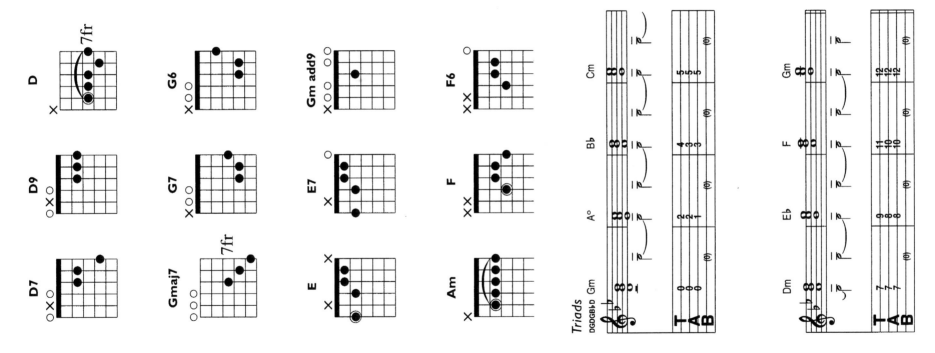

58

Two-note voicings

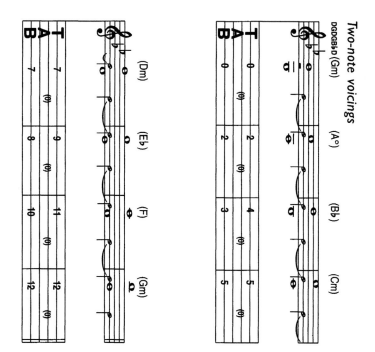

DGDGB♭D (Gm)

(A°)　(B♭)　(Cm)

(Dm)　(E♭)　(F)　(Gm)

(A°)

Melody in Gm

Very slowly

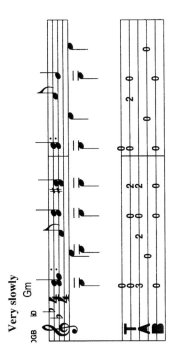
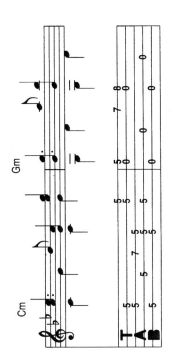
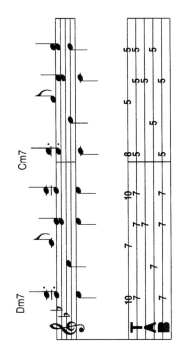
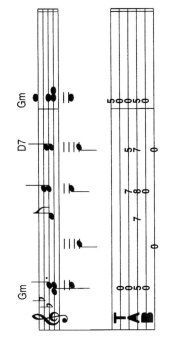

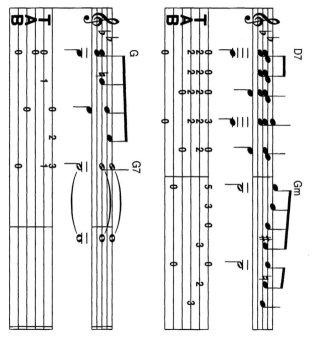
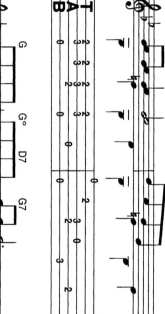
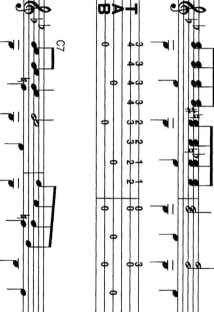
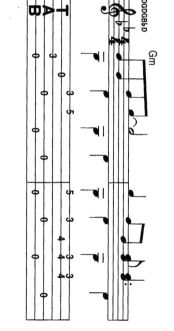

BLUES IN SPANISH MINOR

RELATED TUNINGS

Open A minor E A E A C E

This tuning has the same interval string relationship as open G minor. Each string is pitched up one whole-step—therefore all the chord blocks, scales, and tablature are fingered the same way.

How to tune from standard:

1
2 raise one half-step to C
3 raise one whole-step to A
4 raise one whole-step to E
5
6

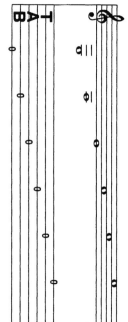

Open A minor tuning staff
EAEACE

OPEN C G C G C E

The open strings in open C tuning, like those in open D, form a major chord with the root on the low sixth string. The difference between the two is that the string relationships within the tuning are not the same—so the open chord is *voiced* differently. The large interval distance between the low C (sixth string) and the high E (first string) makes this a particularly rich and full sounding tuning. I wrote out an arrangement of "Amazing Grace" to illustrate how beautifully a melody and chords can move within this tuning.

How to tune from standard:

1
2 raise one half-step to C
3
4 lower one whole-step to C
5 lower one whole-step to G
6 lower two whole-step to C

Open C tuning staff
CGCGCE

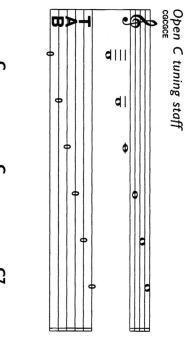

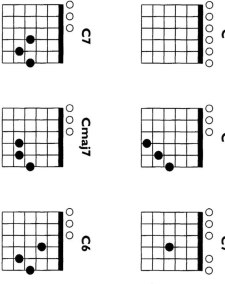

C   C   C7

C7   Cmaj7   C6

65

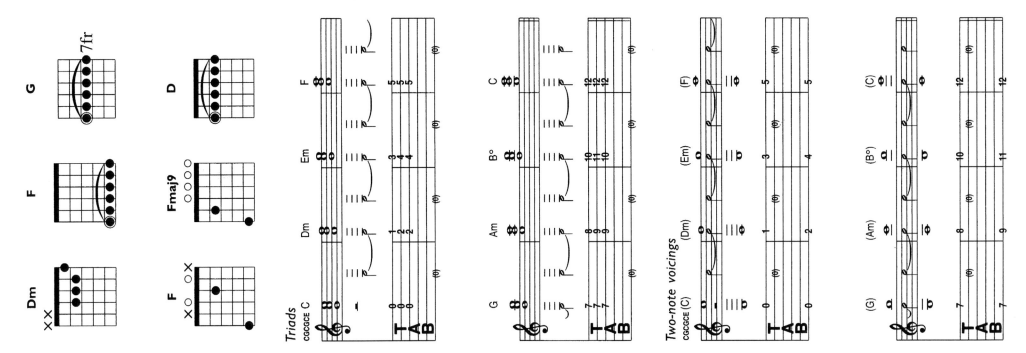

66

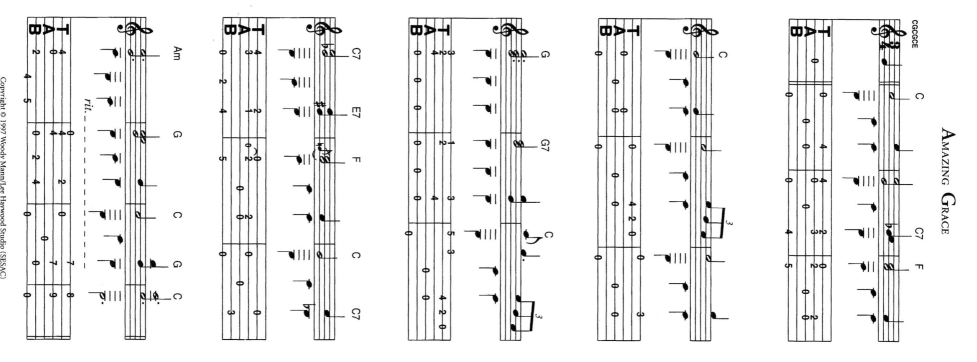

67

Drop C C A D G B E

By lowering the sixth string one whole-step to C, songs in the key of C can now have the strong the root tone in the bass. Play all the chord blocks on the top five strings the same way as in standard tuning.

How to tune from standard:

1
2
3
4
5
6 lower two whole-steps to C

Drop C tuning staff
CADGBE

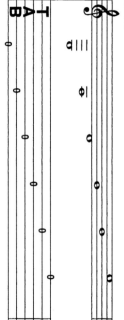

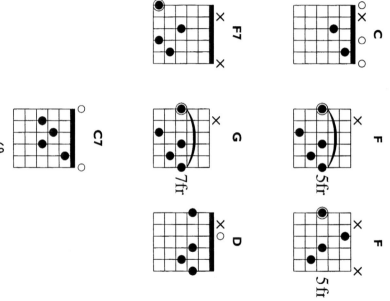

69

Drop CG C G D G B E

This tuning has the sixth and fifth strings as C and G—so it is a logical choice for tunes in either the key of C or G so I notated the basic chords in both keys. Notice that all of the chord formations on the top four strings have the same fingering as they do in standard tuning. This tuning is also used by many Hawaiian guitar players.

How to tune from standard:

1
2
3
4
5 lower one whole-step to G
6 lower two whole-steps to C

Drop CG tuning staff
CGDGBE

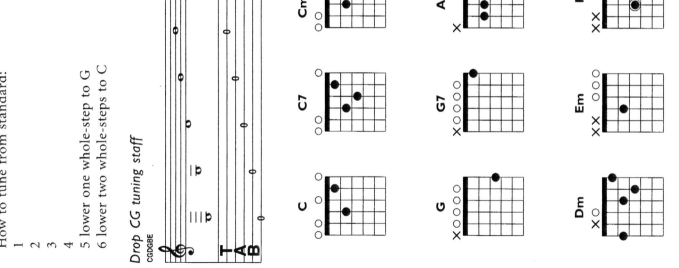

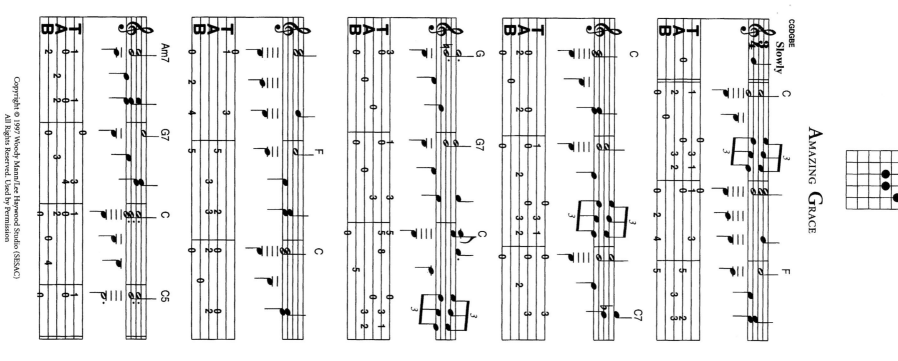

Amazing Grace

C Spanish C G D G B D

This is the same as open G (Spanish) tuning except that the low string is a C instead of a D–so you can use many of the same chord formations and riffs as you would in open G. *C Spanish* also works well when you're playing in the keys of C or G. For example, when playing a blues in G, the lowered sixth string to C provides the solid root tone of the IV chord. This is also a favorite tuning among Hawaiian musicians when playing songs in the key of C.

How to tune from standard:
1 lower one whole-step to D
2
3
4
5 lower one whole-step to G
6 lower two whole-steps to C

Drop C Spanish tuning staff
CGDGBD

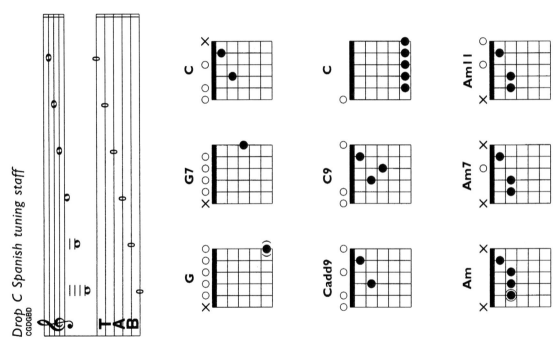

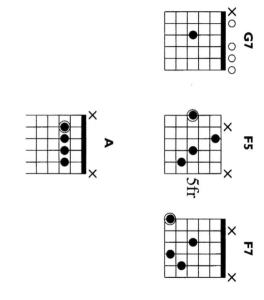

74

The following is a blues in the key of G. This way I can use the low C note as the root of the IV chord (C).

Blues in Spanish C

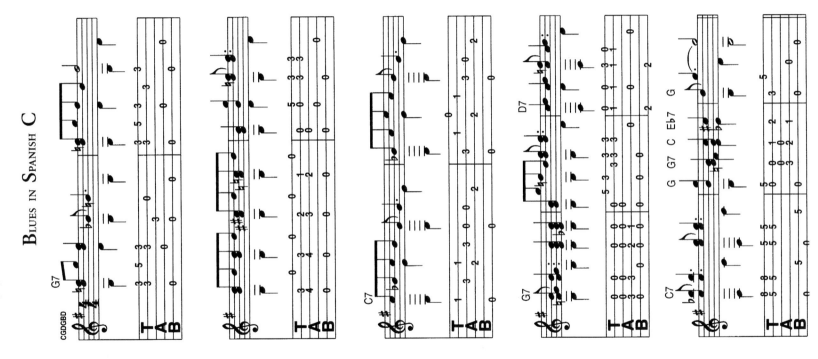

C G D G A D

Here's another tuning that can imply more than one tonality. This is sort of a drop CG–DADGAD. The chords positions on the top four strings are the same as in DADGAD .

How to tune from standard:
1 lower one whole-step to D
2 lower one whole-step to A
3
4
5 lower one whole-step to G
6 lower two whole-steps to C

CGDGAD tuning staff

CGDGAD

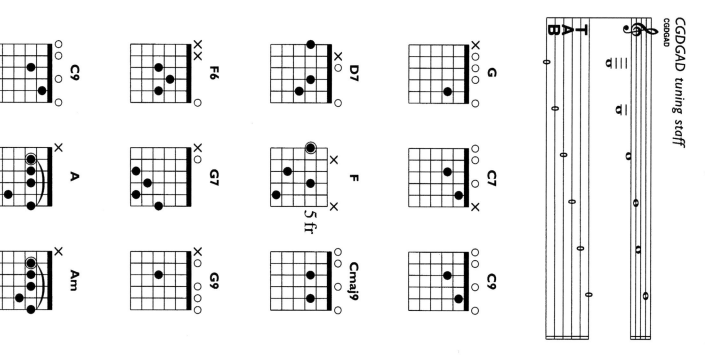

C G C G A E

This tuning is part of a group of Hawaiian tunings that have the first and second string tuned a fifth (or fourth) apart. They are called the *Mauna Loa* tunings. The open strings in this C tonality tuning form a major 6 chord.

How to tune from standard:

1
2 lower one whole-step to A
3
4 lower one whole-step to C
5 lower one whole-step to G
6 lower two whole-steps to C

CGCGAE tuning staff

CGCGAE

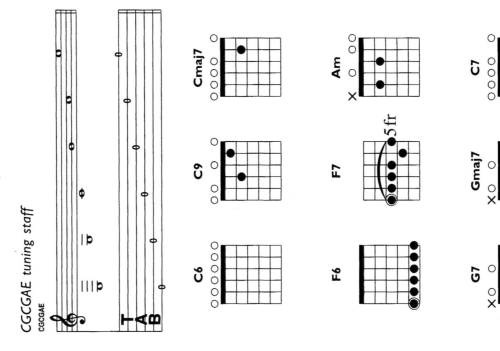

Cmaj7

C9

C6

Am

F7   5 fr

F6

C7

Gmaj7

G7

Fmaj7

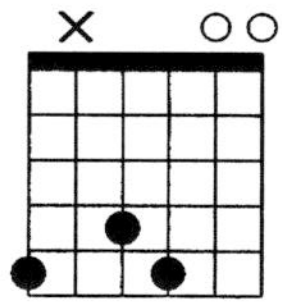

Cm6

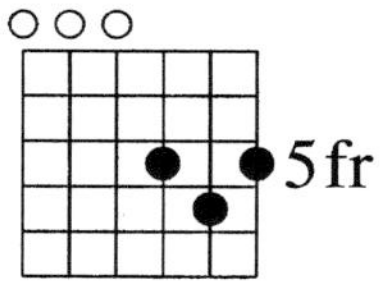

C

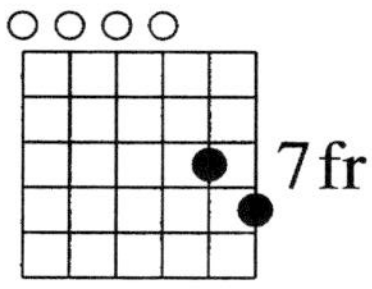

G6

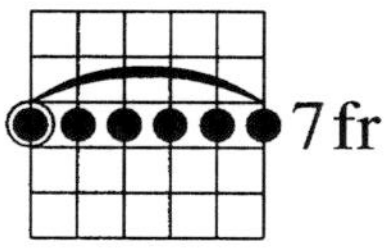

G9 7fr

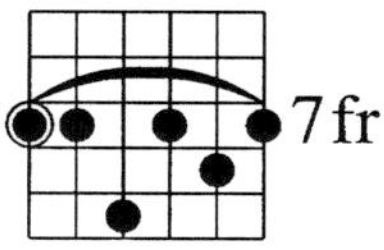

Dm7

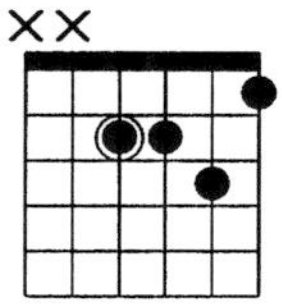

Cm 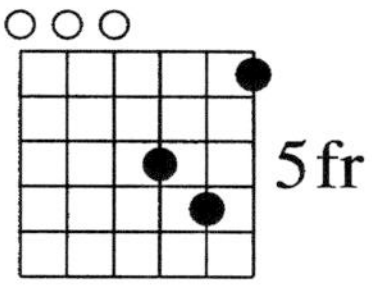 5fr

F7 5fr

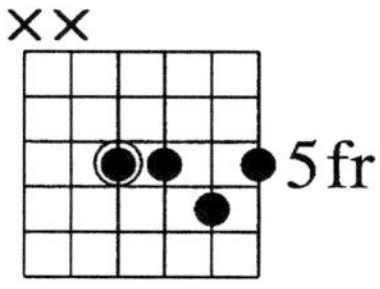

C7 7fr

5fr

7fr

7fr

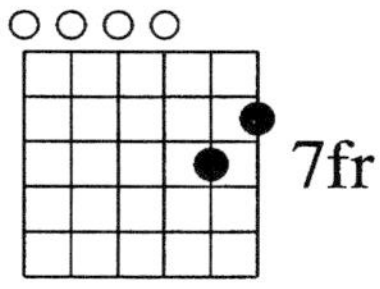

OPEN C MINOR

C G G C E♭

Like open C (major) this tuning has a wide interval distance between the first and sixth string. With the root of the chord in the bass it forms a full, rich C minor chord.

How to tune from standard:
1 lower one half-step to E♭
2 raise one half-step to C
3
4 lower one whole-step to C
5 lower one whole-step to G
6 lower two whole-steps to C

Open C minor tuning staff
CGGCE♭

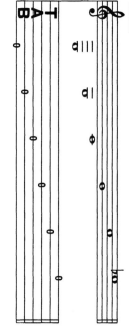

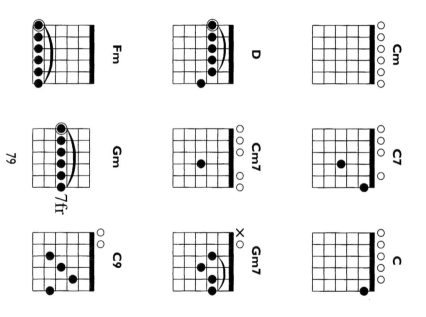

79

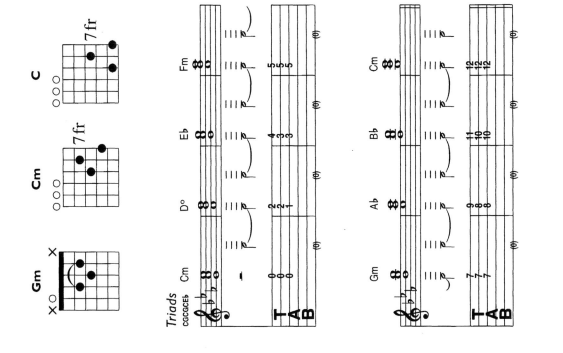

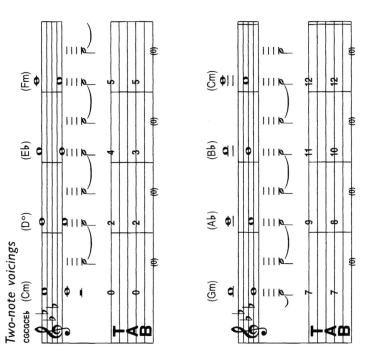

Triads

Two-note voicings

C Minor Waltz

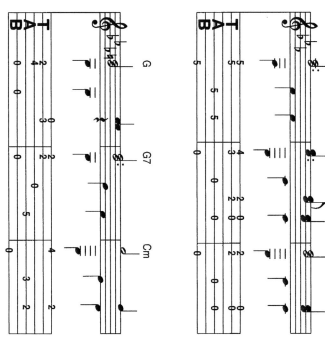

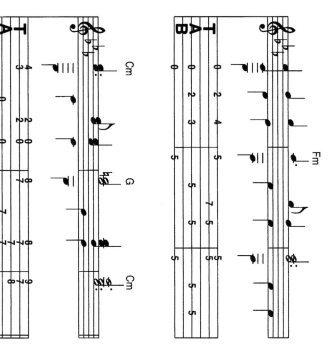

FURTHER POSSIBILITIES

Lute Tuning E A D F♯ B E

To tune from standard:

1
2
3 lower one half-step to F♯
4
5
6

Perfect 4th Tuning E A D G C F

To tune:

1 raise one half-step to F
2 raise one half-step to C
3
4
5
6

OPEN CHORD TUNINGS

D7 D A D F♯ C D

1 lower one whole-step to D
2 raise one half-step to C
3 lower one half-step to F♯
4
5
6 lower one whole-step to D

G7 D G D F B D

1 lower one whole-step to D
2
3 lower one whole-step to F
4
5 lower one whole-step to G
6 lower one whole-step to D

Gmaj7 D G D F♯ B D

1 lower one whole-step to D
2
3 lower one half-step to F♯
4
5 lower one whole-step to G
6 lower one whole-step to D

Dmaj7 D A D F♯ A C♯

1 lower one whole-step and a half to C♯
2 lower one whole-step to A
3 lower one half-step to F♯
4
5
6 lower one whole-step to D

Gm7 D G D F B♭ D

1 lower one whole-step to D
2 lower one half-step to B♭
3 lower one whole-step to F
4
5 lower one whole-step to G
6 lower one whole-step to D

85

Dm7 D A D F A C

1 lower two whole-steps to C
2 lower one whole-step to A
3 lower one whole-step to F
4
5
6 lower one whole-step to D

Am7 E A E G C E

1
2 raise one half-step to C
3
4 raise one whole-step to E
5
6

Em7 E B D G B E

1
2
3
4
5 raise one whole-step to B
6

Two-Note Tunings

D A D D A D

1 lower one whole-step to D
2 lower one whole-step to A
3 lower two whole-steps and a half to D
4
5
6 lower one whole-step to D

D G D D G D

1 lower one whole-step to D
2 lower two whole-steps to G
3 lower two whole-steps and a half to D
4
5 lower one whole-step to G
6 lower one whole-step to D

E A E E A E

1
2 lower one whole-step to A
3 lower two whole-steps and a half to E
4 raise on whole-step to E
5
6

E B E E B E

1
2
3 lower two whole-steps and a half to E
4 raise one whole-step to E
5 raise one whole-step to B

Discography

Listening to some of the following recordings will give you an idea of how guitarists use alternate tunings in a variety of styles. This listing includes contemporary artists as well as many of the early innovators who established the use of open tunings as a workable alternative to standard. It is by no means meant to be the complete list, and the categorizing of the musicians is to simply organize the references—in case you are unfamiliar with any of the names. Also listed, at the end, are anthology recordings that highlight artists who used open tunings extensively.

Traditional Country Blues

Kokomo Arnold
DADF#AD (Open D)

"Milk Cow Blues"
The Roots of Robert Johnson (Yazoo)

"Mean Old Twister"
Kokomo Arnold (Classics-Arhoolie)

Barbecue Bob
DGDGBD (Open G)

"Yo Yo Blues"
Chocolate to the Bone (Yazoo)

"Its Just Too Bad"
Chocolate to the Bone (Yazoo)

Bo Carter
DGDGBD (Drop DG)

"I Want You to Know"
Bo Carter's Greatest Hits (Yazoo)

"Who's Been Here?"
Bo Carter's Greatest Hits (Yazoo)

Clifford Gibson
DGDGBD (Open G)

"Tired of Being Mistreated"
Beat You Doing It (Yazoo)

"Beat You Doing It"
Beat You Doing It (Yazoo)

"Stop Your Rambling"
Beat You Doing It (Yazoo)

Buddy Boy Hawkins
DGDGBD (Open G)

"Snatch It and Grab It"
Buddy Boy Hawkins and His Buddies 1927–1934 (Yazoo)

"Voice Throwin' Blues"
Buddy Boy Hawkins and His Buddies 1927–1934 (Yazoo)

King Solomon Hill
DADF#AD (Open D)

"Whoopee Blues"
Bottleneck Blues Guitar Classics 1926–1937 (Yazoo)

"The Gone Dead Train"
Tex-Arkana-Louisiana Country 1927–1932 (Yazoo)

Son House
DGDGBD (Open G)

"Dry Spell Blues"
Masters of the Delta Blues (Yazoo)

"Country Farm Blues"
Son House: The Complete Library of Congress Sessions (Travelin' Man)

"Levee Blues"
Son House: The Complete Library of Congress Sessions (Travelin' Man)

"Special Rider Blues"
Son House: The Complete Library of Congress Sessions (Travelin' Man)

"Walking Blues"
Son House: The Complete Library of Congress Sessions (Travelin' Man)

Bo Weavil Jackson
DADF#AD (Open D)

"You Can't Keep No Brown"
Bottleneck Blues Guitar Classics (Yazoo)

Elmore James
DADF#AD (Open D)

"Dust My Broom"
Who's Muddy Shoes (Chess)

Skip James
DADFAD (Open D minor)

"Devil Got My Woman"
The Complete Early Recordings of Skip James—1930 (Yazoo)

"Hard Time Killin' Floor Blues"
The Complete Early Recordings of Skip James—1930 (Yazoo)

DGDGBD (Open G)

"Special Rider"
The Complete Early Recordings of Skip James—1930 (Yazoo)

Lonnie Johnson
DGDGBE (Drop DG)

"Away Down the Alley Blues"
Eddie Lang and Lonnie Johnson (Swagghie)

"Life Saver Blues"
The Roots of Robert Johnson (Yazoo)

"Mean Old Bedbug Blues"
Lonnie Johnson—Steppin' on the Blues (Columbia)

"Playing with the Strings"
Lonnie Johnson—Steppin' on the Blues (Columbia)

"Have to Change Keys"
Lonnie Johnson—Steppin' on the Blues (to Play These Blues) (Columbia)

"Deep Blue Sea Blues"
Lonnie Johnson—Steppin' on the Blues (Columbia)

Robert Johnson
DGDGBD (Open G)

"Come on in My Kitchen"
The Complete Recordings (Columbia)

"Crossroad Blues"
The Complete Recordings (Columbia)

"Milkcow's Calf Blues"
The Complete Recordings (Columbia)

"Terraplane Blues"
The Complete Recordings (Columbia)

"Walking Blues"
The Complete Recordings (Columbia)

DADF#AD (Open D)

"Preachin' Blues"
The Complete Recordings (Columbia)

"Hell Hound on My Trail"
The Complete Recordings (Columbia)

"Ramblin' on My Mind"
The Complete Recordings (Columbia)

DADGBE (Drop D)

"I Believe I'll Dust My Broom"
The Complete Recordings (Columbia)

"Malted Milk"
The Complete Recordings (Columbia)

Blind Willie Johnson
DADF♯AD (Open D)

"God Moves on the Water"
Praise God I'm Satisfied (Yazoo)

"Dark Was the Night—Cold Was the Ground"
Praise God I'm Satisfied (Yazoo)

"Nobody's Fault but Mine"
Praise God I'm Satisfied (Yazoo)

Fred McDowell
DADF♯AD (Open D)

"You Got to Move"
Mississippi Delta Blues (Arhoolie)

Memphis Minnie
DGDGBD (Open G)

"Me and My Chauffeur"
I Ain't No Bad Girl (Portrait - out of print)

Willie Newburn
DGDGBD (Open G)

"Roll and Tumble"
Roots of Robert Johnson (Yazoo)

Charlie Patton
DADF♯AD (Open D)

"A Spoonful Blues"
Founder of the Delta Blues (Yazoo)

EAEAC♯E (Open A)

"High Sheriff Blues"
Founder of the Delta Blues (Yazoo)

DGDGBD (Open G)

"Mississippi Bo Weavil"
Founder of the Delta Blues (Yazoo)

"Screamin' and Hollerin' the Blues"
Founder of the Delta Blues (Yazoo)

"Moon Going Down"
Founder of the Delta Blues (Yazoo)

"Revenue Man"
King of the Delta Blues (Yazoo)

Tampa Red
DADF♯AD (Open D)

"You Got to Reap What You Sow"
Tampa Red Bottleneck Guitar (1928–1937) (Yazoo)

"Denver Blues"
Tampa Red Bottleneck Guitar (1928–1937) (Yazoo)

"If You Want Me to Love You"
Tampa Red Bottleneck Guitar (1928–1937) (Yazoo)

"Boogie Woogie Dance"
Guitar Wizards 1926-1935 (Yazoo)

Henry Townsend
EBEGBE (Open E minor)

"Mistreated Blues"
St. Louis Blues (Yazoo)

Muddy Waters
DGDGBD (Open G)

"I Be's Troubled"
Muddy Waters Down on Stovall's Plantation (Testament)

"I Feel Like Going Home"
Muddy Waters Down on Stovall's Plantation (Testament)

"Louisiana Blues"
Muddy Waters Down on Stovall's Plantation (Testament)

"Rollin' and Tumblin'"
Muddy Waters Down on Stovall's Plantation (Testament)

"Streamline Woman"
Muddy Waters Down on Stovall's Plantation (Testament)

Other recordings that are more readily available:

Muddy Waters: The Complete Plantation Records (Chess/MCA)

Muddy Waters: The Chess Box (Chess)

Booker 'Bukka' White
DADF#AD (Open D)

"Jitterbug Swing"
The Complete Sessions 1930–1940 (Travelin' Man)

"The Panama Limited"
The Complete Sessions 1930–1940 (Travelin' Man)

DGDGBD (Open G)

"Fixin' to Die"
The Complete Sessions 1930–1940 (Travelin' Man)

Anthologies

Bottleneck Blues Guitar Classics 1926–1937 (Yazoo)
Bottleneck Guitar Trendsetters of the 1930s (Yazoo)
Guitar Wizards 1926–1935 (Yazoo)
The Roots of Robert Johnson (Yazoo)
The Slide Guitar: Bottles, Knives, & Steel (Columbia)
The Slide Guitar: Bottles, Knives, & Steel, Vol. 2 (Columbia)

Hawaiian

Keola Beamer

CGDGBD (C Wahine)

"Hemo Da Kope Bean"
Wooden Boat (Dancing Cat)

"Po Mahina"
Wooden Boat (Dancing Cat)

"Wooden Boat"
Wooden Boat (Dancing Cat)

"Don't You Want to Be My Baby"
Wooden Boat (Dancing Cat)

CGCGAD

"Ku'u Morning Dew"
Moe 'Uhane Kika (Dancing Cat)

"Dancers in the Land of Po"
Wooden Boat (Dancing Cat)

CFCGAF

"Elepanio Slack Key"
Wooden Boat (Dancing Cat)

Sonny Chillingworth

DGDGBD (Taro Patch)

"Moe 'Uhane"
Sonny Solo (Dancing Cat)

"Kaula 'ili"
Sonny Solo (Dancing Cat)

"Wai Ulu"
Sonny Solo (Dancing Cat)

CGDGBD (C Wahine)

"Pua Liliehua"
Sonny Solo (Dancing Cat)

"Hi'ilawe"
Sonny Solo (Dancing Cat)

"Hula Medley"
Sonny Solo (Dancing Cat)

DGDF#BD (G Wahine)

"Charmarita/Malasadas"
Sonny Solo (Dancing Cat)

DGDDGD (G Mauna loa)

"Papakolea"
Sonny Solo (Dancing Cat)

DGDEGD

"Maori Brown Eyes"
Sonny Solo (Dancing Cat)

FGCGAE

"Let Me Hear You Whisper"
Sonny Solo (Dancing Cat)

Ray Kane

DGDGBD (Taro Patch)

"Wai'anae Slack Key Hula"
Punahele (Dancing Cat)

"Kealoha"
Punahele (Dancing Cat)

"E Hulihuli Ho'i Mai"
Punahele (Dancing Cat)

"Mauna Loa"
Punahele (Dancing Cat)

CGDGBD (C Wahine)

"Pua Makahala"
Punahele (Dancing Cat)

"Mai'Ae I Ka Hewa"
Punahele (Dancing Cat)

DADF#AC# (D Wahine)

"Nani Ho'omana'o"
Punahele (Dancing Cat)

DGDF#BD (G Wahine)

"Punahele"
Punahele (Dancing Cat)

Leonard Kwan

CGDGBD (C Wahine)

"Ke'ala's Mele"
Ke'ala's Mele (Dancing Cat)

Gabby Pahinui

CGEGAE

"No Ke Ano Ahiahi"
An Island Heritage (Panini Records)

Cyril Pahinui

CGEGCE (C major)

"Panini Pua Kea"
6 & 12 String Slack Key (Dancing Cat)

"Moani Ke 'Ala"
6 & 12 String Slack Key (Dancing Cat)

"Hilo E"
6 & 12 String Slack Key (Dancing Cat)

"Lei 'Ohu"
6 & 12 String Slack Key (Dancing Cat)

"Hanauma Bay"
6 & 12 String Slack Key (Dancing Cat)

"No Ke Ano Ahiahi"
6 & 12 String Slack Key (Dancing Cat)

CGEGAE (C Mauna Loa)

"Noenoe"
6 & 12 String Slack Key (Dancing Cat)

DADF#BE (D major)

"Marketplace"
6 & 12 String Slack Key (Dancing Cat)

"Moloka'i-nui-a-Hina"
6 & 12 String Slack Key (Dancing Cat)

"Lullaby for Pops"
6 & 12 String Slack Key (Dancing Cat)

Anthologies

Hawaiian Slack Key Guitar Masters: Instrumental Masters (Dancing Cat)

Hawaiian Steel Guitar (Arhoolie)

Slack Key Giants (Pume)

Celtic

Pierre Bensusan
FGDGCF

"Près de Paris/Reels"
Près de Paris (Rounder)

DADGAD

"Jigs: Merrily Kissed the Quaker/Cunla"
Près de Paris (Rounder)

"March: The Return from Fingal"
Pierre Bensusan 2 (Rounder)

"Water Music (G.F.Handel)"
Musique (Rounder)

"Suite flamande aux pommes"
Solilai (Rounder)

"The Last Pint"
Spices (Rounder)

"Autour du jour en 80 mondes"
Wu Wei (Rounder)

Davey Graham
DADGAD

"She Moved thro' the Fair"
Folk, Blues & Beyond (Deram/Decca)

EADEAE

"Lord Mayo/Lord Inchiquin"
Music of Ireland (Shanachie)

"The Frieze Britches"
Music of Ireland (Shanachie)

"Hardiman the Fiddler"
Music of Ireland (Shanachie)

Bert Jansch
DADGBE (Drop D)

"Black Water Side"
Jack Orion (Demon/Transatlantic)

DADGAD
DADGCE
"So Long (Been on the Road So Long)"
It Don't Bother Me (Demon/Transatlantic)

John Renbourn

DADGAD
"Lamento di Tristan—Rotta"
The Lady and the Unicorn (Shanachie)

DGDGCD
"Altarello"
The Lady and the Unicorn (Shanachie))
"Trotto"
The Lady and the Unicorn (Shanachie)

DADGAD
"Lindsay"
Live in America (Flying Fish)
"Sandwood Down to Kyle"
Ship of Fools (Flying Fish)

DADGBE (Drop D)
"Toy for Two Lutes"
The Hermit (Shanachie)

"Lord Inchiquin"
The Hermit (Shanachie)

"Mrs. O'Rourke"
The Hermit (Shanachie)

"Lady Nothynge's Toye Puffe"
Another Monday (Essential /Castle)

DADGBD (Double drop D)
"The South Wind"
Wheel of Fortune (Flying Fish)

DGDGBD (Open G)
"The English Dance"
The Black Baloon (Shanachie)
"The Blarney Pilgrim"
Wheel of Fortune (Flying Fish)
"Bunyan's Hymn"
Wheel of Fortune (Flying Fish)
"I Saw Three Ships"
Wheel of Fortune (Flying Fish)

DGDGBbD (Open G minor)
"Mist Covered Mountains of Home"
The Black Baloon (Shanachie)
"Lamentation for Owen Roe O'Neill"
The Hermit (Shanachie)
"The Moon Shines Bright"
The Black Baloon (Shanachie)
"The Orphan"
The Black Baloon (Shanachie)

CGGGCF

"Bouree I/Bouree II"
The Hermit (Shanachie)

FCCGCF

"Gipsy's Dance/Jews' Dance"
A Maid in Bedlam (Shanachie)

Anthologies

Celtic Connections (The Living Tradition)

Evolving Tradition (Mrs. Casey's Records)

Evolving Tradition 2 (Mrs. Casey's Records)

Flight of the Green Linnet (Rycodisc)

Irish Reels, Jigs, Airs, and Hornpipes (Schanachie)

Music of Ireland (Schanachie)

The Best of and the Rest of Folk Masters
   (Action Reply Records)

The Celts Rise Again (Green Linnet)

The Folk Collection (Topic)

The Folk Collection 2 (Topic)

The Music of O'Carolan (Schanachie)

Rock, Folk, and the Contemporary Stylists

The Allman Brothers Band
EBEG♯BE (Open E)

"Little Martha"
Eat a Peach (Polydor)

Chet Atkins
DGDGBE (Drop DG)

"Yellow Bird"
This Is Chet Atkins (Columbia)

DADGBE (Drop D)

"Londonderry Air"
Alone (Columbia)

EAC♯GBE

"Honolulu Blue"
Street Dreams (Columbia)

DGDGBE (Drop DG)

"Both Sides Now"
This Is Chet Atkins (Columbia)

The Beatles
DADGBE (Drop D)

"Dear Prudence"
The White Album (Capitol)

Jeff Beck

DADF#AD (Open D)

"Loser"
Mellow Gold (Epic)

Black Crowes

DGDGBD (Open G)

"Gone"
Amorica (American Recordings)
"Cursed Diamond"
Amorica (American Recordings)
"Downtown Money Waster"
Amorica (American Recordings)
"Hotel Illness"
Southern Harmony & Musical Companion
(American Recordings)

FBbFBbDF

"Nonfiction"
Amorica (American Recordings)

Martin Carthy

DADEAE

"Peggy and the Soldier"
Martin Carthy: Second Album (Topic)
"Byker Hill"
Byker Hill (Topic)
"Polly on the Shore"
Prince Heathen (Topic)
"Cold, Haily, Windy Night"
Landfall (Topic)

DGCGCD

"The Famous Flower of Serving Men"
Shearwater (Mooncrest)

CGCDGA

"Cold, Haily, Windy Night"
Because It's There (Topic)

DADC#AC#

"Sovay"
The Complete Brass Monkey (Topic)

CGCDGA

"The Handweaver and the Factory Maid"
The Complete Brass Monkey (Topic)

Eric Clapton

DADF#AD (Open D)

"Nobody Knows You When You're Down and Out"
Derek and the Dominos: 20th Anniversary (Polydor)

DADF#AD (Open D)

"Blues Before Sunrise"
From the Cradle (Reprise)

DGDGBD (Open G)

"Running on Faith"
Unplugged (Reprise)

"Walkin' Blues"
Unplugged (Reprise)

"Rollin' and Tumblin'"
Unplugged (Reprise)

Shawn Colvin
DGDGBD (Open G)

"Steady On"
Steady On (Columbia)

"Tenderness on the Block"
Fat City (Columbia)

"Object of My Desire"
Fat City (Columbia)

DADGBE (Drop D)

"Shotgun Down the Avalanche"
Steady On (Columbia)

"Polaroids"
Fat City (Columbia)

"Kill the Messenger"
Fat City (Columbia)

"This Must Be the Place"
Cover Girl (Columbia)

DADGBD (Double drop D)

"Diamond in the Rough"
Steady On (Columbia)

CGDGBbD

"Orion in the Sky"
Fat City (Columbia)

"Tennessee"
Fat City (Columbia)

Albert Collins
FCFACF (Open F minor)

"Frosty"
Frozen Alive (Alligator)

Ry Cooder
DADGBE (Drop D)

"FDR in Trinidad"
Into the Purple Valley (Reprise)

"Great Dream from Heaven"
Into the Purple Valley (Reprise)

"Vigilante Man"
Into the Purple Valley (Reprise)
DADF♯AD (Open D)
"Thirteen Question Method"
Get Rhythm (Reprise)
DGDGBD (Open G)
"Available Space"
Available Space (Reprise)

Crosby, Stills & Nash
EEEEBE
"Suite Judy Blue Eyes"
Crosby, Stills & Nash (Atlantic)
EBDGAD
"Guinnevere"
Crosby, Stills & Nash (Atlantic)
E♭B♭FGB♭E♭ (Open E♭)
"Lady of the Island"
Crosby, Stills & Nash (Atlantic)

Crosby, Stills, Nash & Young
E♭E♭E♭E♭B♭E♭
"Carry On"
Déjà Vu (Atlantic)
EEEEBE
"4+20"
Déjà Vu (Atlantic)
DADGBE (Drop D)
"Teach Your Children"
Déjà Vu (Atlantic)

Alex de Grassi
DADGBE (Drop D)
"Children's Dance"
Turning: Turning Back (Windham Hill)
DGAADD
"Mirage"
Deep at Night (Windham Hill)
DGBAEE
"Slow Circle II"
Slow Circle (Windham Hill)
E♭GACDD
"Western"
Southern Exposure (Windham Hill)
EF♯BBEE
"Turning"
Turning: Turning Back (Windham Hill)

"Causeway"
Slow Circle (Windham Hill)

FGACDD

"McCormick"
Antiplano (Windham Hill)

"Southern Exposure"
Southern Exposure (Windham Hill)

John Fahey
DADF#AD (Open D)

"Poor Boy Long Ways From Home"
The Legend of Blind Joe Death (Takoma)

DGDGBD (Open G)

"The First Noel"
Christmas Guitar (Varrick/Rounder)

"On the Sunny Side of the Ocean"
Return of the Repressed: The John Fahey Anthology (Rhino)

"Spanish Two-Step"
Return of the Repressed: The John Fahey Anthology (Rhino)

CGCGCE (Open C)

"Joy to the World"
Christmas Guitar (Varrick/Rounder)

"Auld Lang Syne"
Christmas Guitar (Varrick/Rounder)

"The Revolt of the Dyke Brigade"
Return of the Repressed: The John Fahey Anthology (Rhino)

"Requiem for John Hurt"
The Essential John Fahey (Vanguard)

Nanci Griffith
DGDGBD (Open G)

"These Bays in the Open Book"
Flyer (Columbia)

"On Grafton Street"
Flyer (Columbia)

"Goodnight to a Mother's Dream"
Flyer (Columbia)

"Nobody's Angel"
Flyer (Columbia)

Buddy Guy
DADGBE (Drop D)

"Buddy's Groove"
Buddy Guy: The Complete Chess Studio Recordings

Richie Havens

DADF#AC (Open D7)

"High Flying Bird"
Mixed Bag (Polydor)

DADF#AD (Open D)

"Handsome Johnny"
Mixed Bag (Polydor)

"Just Like a Woman"
Mixed Bag (Polydor)

"Freedom"
Woodstock (Warners)

"Here Comes the Sun"
The Great Blind Degree (Stormy Forest)

Michael Hedges

BADEAB

"The Root Witch"
Taproot (Windham Hill)

CCDGAD

"Breakfast in the Field"
Breakfast in the Field (Windham Hill)

"Aerial Boundries"
Aerial Boundries (Windham Hill)

CGDGGG

"Rickover's Dream"
Aerial Boundries (Windham Hill) CCDGAD

"Bensusan"
Aerial Boundries (Windham Hill)

DADGCC

"Watching My Life Go By"
Watching My Life Go By (Windham Hill)

"Ritual Dance"
Taproot (Windham Hill)

DAEEAA

"All Along the Watchtower"
Watching My Life Go By (Windham Hill)

DAEFAE

"Oracle"
Oracle (Windham Hill)

John Lee Hooker

EAEAC#E (Open A)

"I Need Some Money"
That's My Story (Fantasy)

"How Can You Do It"
That's My Story (Fantasy)

"How Long Blues"
Country Blues of John Lee Hooker (Fantasy)

DGDGBD (Open G)

"I Need Some Money"
That's My Story (Fantasy)

"Democrat Man"
That's My Story (Fantasy)

DGDFAD (Open G9)

"I'm Workin'"
That's My Story (Fantasy)

Leo Kottke
AEAEAC♯ (Open C tuned down to A)

"Busted Bicycle"
6 & 12 String Guitar (Takoma)

DGDGBD (Open G)

"Jesu, Joy of Man's Desiring"
6 & 12 String Guitar (Takoma)

DADGBE (Drop D)

"Mona Ray"
My Father's Face (Private Music)

"William Powell"
My Father's Face (Private Music)

Led Zeppelin
DADGAD

"Black Mountain Song"
Led Zeppelin (Atlantic)

"Kashmir"
Physical Graffiti (Swan Song)

DGDGBD (Open G)

"Going to California"
Led Zeppelin III (Atlantic)

DGCGCD

"The Rain Song"
Houses of the Holy (Atlantic)

CACGCE

"Bron-Y-Aur"
Led Zeppelin III (Atlantic)

Joni Mitchell
DGDGBD (Open G)

"Marcie"
Joni Mitchell (Reprise)

"The Circle Game"
Ladies of the Canyon (Reprise)

DADF♯AD (Open D)

"You Turn Me On, I'm a Radio"
For the Roses (Asylum)

DAEF#AE
"Cherokee Louise"
Night Ride Home (Geffen)

DADGBD
"Free Man in Paris"
Court and Spark (Asylum)

EBEG#BE (Open E)
"Chelsea Morning"
Clouds (Reprise)
"Both Sides Now"
Clouds (Reprise)
"Big Yellow Taxi"
Ladies of the Canyon (Reprise)

CGDGBD
"Cold Blue Steel and Sweet Fire"
For the Roses (Asylum)

CGDFCE
"Woman of Heart and Mind"
For the Roses (Asylum)
"Sisotowbell Lane"
Joni Mitchell (Reprise)
"Just Like This Train"
Court and Spark (Asylum)

"Coyote"
Hejira (Asylum)

"Don Juan's Reckless Daughter"
Don Juan's Reckless Daughter (Asylum)

BF#D#D#F#B
"How Do You Stop?"
Turbulent Indigo (Reprise)
"Borderline"
Turbulent Indigo (Reprise)

BF#BEAE
"The Magdalene Laundries"
Turbulent Indigo (Reprise)

Nirvana
DbAbDbGbAbEb
"Scentless Apprentice"
In Utero (Geffen)
"Heart-Shaped Box"
In Utero (Geffen)

EbAbDbGbBbEb
"Serve the Servants"
In Utero (Geffen)
"Rape Me"
In Utero (Geffen)

"Frances Farmer Will Have Her Way in Seattle"
In Utero (Geffen)

"Milk It"
In Utero (Geffen)

"Dumb"
In Utero (Geffen)

"Very Ape"
In Utero (Geffen)

"Penny Royal Tea"
In Utero (Geffen)

"Radio Friendly Unit Shifter"
In Utero (Geffen)

"Tourette's"
In Utero (Geffen)

DGCFAD

"Come as You Are"
Never Mind (Geffen)

"Lithium"
Never Mind (Geffen)

"Drain You"
Never Mind (Geffen)

CGCFAD

"Something in the Way"
Never Mind (Geffen)

EbBbGbDbBbDb

"Lake of Fire"
MTV Unplugged in New York (Geffen)

"Something in the Way"
MTV Unplugged in New York (Geffen)

Pearl Jam
DADF#AD (Open D)

"Even Flow"
Ten (Epic)

"Oceans"
Ten (Epic)

EAC#EAE

"Serve the Servants"
Ten (Epic)

Bonnie Raitt
EbAbDbGbBbEb

"Someting to Talk About"
Luck of the Draw (Capitol)

The Rolling Stones
DGDGBD (Open G)

"Some Girls"
Some Girls (Rolling Stones/Virgin)

"Before They Make Me Run"
Some Girls (Rolling Stones/Virgin)

"Brown Sugar"
Sticky Fingers (Rolling Stones/Virgin)

"Can't You Hear Me Knockin'"
Sticky Fingers (Rolling Stones/Virgin)

"Rocks Off"
Exile on Main Street (Rolling Stones/Virgin)

"Rip This Joint"
Exile on Main Street (Rolling Stones/Virgin)

"Shake Your Hips (aka *Hip Shake*)"
Exile on Main Street (Rolling Stones/Virgin)

"Casino Boogie"
Exile on Main Street (Rolling Stones/Virgin)

"Tumbling Dice"
Exile on Main Street (Rolling Stones/Virgin)

"Happy"
Exile on Main Street (Rolling Stones/Virgin)

"Hearts for Sale"
Steel Wheels (Rolling Stones/Virgin)

"Mixed Emotions"
Steel Wheels (Rolling Stones/Virgin)

EBEG#BE (Open E)

"Shattered"
Some Girls (Rolling Stones/Virgin)

"Street Fightin' Man"
Beggar's Banquet (Columbia)

DADGBE (Drop D)

"Luving Cup"
Exile on Main Street (Rolling Stones/Virgin)

Paul Simon
DGCFAD

"Late Great Johnny Ace"
Hearts and Bones (WarnerBrothers)

"Peace Like a River"
Paul Simon (Warner Brothers)

Smashing Pumpkins
E♭A♭D♭G♭B♭E♭

"Mayonnaise"
Siamese Dreams (Virgin)

Sonic Youth
BEDDBB

"Bone"
Experimental Jet Set (Geffen)

GGDDE♭E♭

"Brother James"
Bad Moon Rising (Geffen)

"Cotton Crown"
Sister (Geffen)

F#F#GGAA

"Schizophrenia"
Sister (Geffen)

CCEBGD

"Cross the Breeze"
Daydream Nation (Geffen)

EBEEAB

"Eric's Trip"
Daydream Nation (Geffen)

"Kissability"
Goo (Geffen)

CCEBGD

"Disappearer"
Goo (Geffen)

GGDDE♭E♭

"Youth against Fascism"
Dirty (Geffen)

Soundgarden
GGDGBD

"Dusty"
Down on the Upside (A&M)

CGCGGE

"Burden in My Hand"
Down on the Upside (A&M)

"Pretty Noose"
Down on the Upside (A&M)

DGCFAD

"Boot Camp"
Down on the Upside (A&M)

"Overfloater"
Down on the Upside (A&M)

DADGBE (Drop D)

"Rhinosaur"
Down on the Upside (A&M)

"Let Me Drown"
Superunknown (A&M)

"Black Hole Sun"
Superunknown (A&M)

CGCGGE

"Head Down"
Superunknown (A&M)

CGDGBE

"Mailman"
Superunknown (A&M)

Joseph Spence
DADGBE (Drop D)

"Coming in on a Wing and a Prayer"
The Complete Folkways Recordings—1958
(Smithsonian/ Folkways)

"There Will Be a Happy Meeting in Glory"
The Complete Folkways Recordings—1958
(Smithsonian/ Folkways)

"Down by the Riverside"
Glory (Rounder)

"Out on the Rolling Sea"
Glory (Rounder)

Stephen Stills
DADGBE (Drop D)

"Bluebird"
Buffalo Springfield (Atco)

CGCEGC

"Love the One You're With"
Stephen Stills (Atlantic)

EEEEBE

"Bluesman"
Manassas (Atlantic)

Richard Thompson
DADGAD

"Banish Misfortune"
Strict Tempo (Hannibal)

FGDGCD

"When the Spell Is Broken"
Across a Crowded Room (Polydor)

DADGBE (Drop D)

"Maggie Cameron"
Watching the Dark (Hannibal)

"Dargai"
Pour Down Like Silver (Hannibal)

"Jenny Lind"
Across a Crowded Room (Polydor)

"Rockin' in Rhythm"
Strict Tempo (Hannibal)

DGDGBD (Open G)

"I Want to See Bright Lights Tonight"
I Want to See Bright Lights Tonight (Hannibal)

"Don't Let a Thief into Your Heart"
First Light (Hannibal)

"Limo Wreck"
Superunknown (A&M)

CGDGBE
"1952 Vincent Black Lightning"
Rumour and Sigh (Capitol)

Neil Young
DADGBD (Double drop D)

"Cinnamon Girl"
Everybody Knows This Is Nowhere (Reprise)

"Down Let It Bring You Down"
After the Gold Rush (Reprise)

Anthologies

A Selection from the Penguin Book of English Folk Songs (Fellside Records)

Folk Heritage (Music Club)

The Best of and the Rest of Folk Masters (Action Reply Records)

The Art of Fingerstyle Guitar (Schanachie)

Troubadours of British Folk—Vols. 1, 2, 3 (Rhino)

Windham Hill: The First Ten Years (Windham Hill)

While many of the recordings listed in the discography have been released on major labels, others have been released by independent companies whose releases may be harder to find away from large cities. We have provided their names and addresses below, or those of distributors and mail order sources.

Dancing Cat Records
Dept. SK
P.O. Box 639
Santa Cruz, CA 95061
USA

Rykodisc/Hannibal
Earful USA
530 North 3rd Street
Minneapolis, MN 55401
USA

Rykodisc/Hannibal
Earful Europe
Unit 3, Linen House
253 Kilburn Lane
London W10 4BQ
UK

Green Linnet Records
43 Beaver Brook Road
Danbury, CT 06810
USA

Rounder Records
Rounder Mail Order
One Camp Street
North Cambridge, MA 02140
USA

Shanachie
P.O. Box 208
Newton, NJ 07860
USA

Topic Records
Topic Mail Order
50 Stroud Green Street
London N4 3EF
UK

Fantasy Inc.
2600 Tenth Street
Berkeley, CA 94710-9887
USA

Two of the best mail order resources for many of the recordings are:

Elderly Instruments
P.O. Box 14249
Lansing, MI 48901-4249
USA

Tower Records
Mail/Customer Orders
1 Piccadilly Circus
London W1R 8TR
UK

Several other fine, specialized mail order resources are:

Andy's Front Hall
Wormer Road
P.O. Box 307
Voorheesville, NY 12186
USA

Roots & Rhythm
P.O. Box 2216
San Leandro, CA 94577
USA

Tayberry Music
760 Ragin Lane
Rock Hill, SC 29732
USA